Saudi-Iranian Relations
1982 - 1997

Saeed M. Badeeb

Saudi-Iranian Relations
1982 - 1997
Second Edition

Published by
Centre for Arab and Iranian Studies
5 Streatham Street
London WC1A 1JB
UK

A catalogue record of this book
is available from the British Library

ISBN 1-872302-10-6

Designed and printed by Satrap Publishing in London. *www.satrap.co.uk*

To my mother and wife,
for their prayers and patience

The Author

Dr. Saeed M. Badeeb was born in Jeddah, Kingdom of Saudi Arabia. He earned a B.A. in 1971 and an M.A. in 1975 from Karachi University in Pakistan. He received a Master of Philosophy in 1983 and a Ph.D. in 1985 from the George Washington University, USA. From 1972 to 2001, he served in the government of the Kingdom of Saudi Arabia. He has written two other books:
The Saudi-Egyptian Conflict over North Yemen (1962-1970) and *Saudi-Iranian Relations (1932-1982),* the latter being a look at the historical relationship between the two countries.
He is currently head of the Badeeb Centre for Research and Analysis, which is based in Jeddah, Kingdom of Saudi Arabia.

ACKNOWLEDGEMENT

I would like to express my thanks and gratitude to all those who have extended to me their hands and contributed to bring this book to its conclusions. There are those who helped me write this work and those who made it possible for me to publish it.

Among those is Mr. **Ahmad Jaafar Raed**, who enriched me with his information on Iran. Dr. **Misbah Zadeh**, an Iranian who lives in Paris, who clarified me on many of the events. Also thanks to Dr. **David E. Long** who contributed heavily to edit this work and bring it to existence. My deep thanks to Mr. **Evan Hendricks**, who did the proof reading of this book. And my sincere thanks to my two daughters, Effat and Uhud.

But above all, I would like to thank the Almighty Allah (God) for enabling me to finish this work and publish it on the right time.

Jeddah, Saudi Arabia
December 01, 2005

CONTENTS

5. Relations with the African Continent: 1982-1997

ABBREVIATIONS AND ACRONYMS

ACC	Arab Cooperation Council
AIOC	Anglo-Iranian Oil Company
ANO	Abu Nidal Organization
ARAMCO	Arabian American Oil Company
BLM	Bahraini Liberation Movement
BND	German Intelligence Organization
CASOC	California Arabian Standard Oil Company
CENTO	Central Treaty Organization
CIA	Central Intelligence Agency
ECO	Central Economic Organization
EU	European Union
FBI	Federal Bureau of Investigation
FIS	Front for Islamic Salvation
FLB	Saudi Foreign Liaison Bureau
GCC	Gulf Cooperation Council
ICJ	International Court of Justice
KDP	Democratic Kurdish Party
MI6	British Intelligence Service
MOIS	Iranian Intelligence Organization
MOSSAD	Israeli Intelligence Service
NATO	North Atlantic Treaty Organization
OPEC	Organization of Petroleum Exporting Countries
PLFP	Popular Front for the Liberation of Palestine
PLO	Palestinian Liberation Organization
RCO	Regional Cooperation Organization
SAVAK	Iranian Secret Service
SPA	Saudi Press Agency
UAE	United Arab Emirates
UN	United Nations
US	United States

PREFACE

One of the great potential pitfalls of cross-cultural political analysis is that it is all too often limited to gathering all the available written and spoken words of policy makers and opinion makers from another culture, interpolating what likely motives the analyst himself or herself might have had to express such views, and assume that those were the real motives that underlay the resulting policies and the underlying public consensus that was used to justify their formulation. Lack of understanding of foreign cultures and values and the concomitant assumption that all political, economic and social motivation is based on ones own culture and values are virtually universal. It is particularly prevalent between Western and non-Western societies.

It is therefore refreshing when one comes across an analysis of political relationships in an important part of the world that remains unfamiliar to most outsiders by someone who is not only well informed about the subject, Saudi-Iranian relations, but more importantly is a product of the cultural values of the region about which he writes. As a scholar and former senior government servant, Dr. Badeeb not only possesses excellent credentials as a long time observer of Saudi-Iranian relations, but on a number of occasions during his distinguished career, he was a participant in the ongoing shifting tides of those relations, not only bilaterally but also how they played out in relations with third countries. This book picks up from an earlier volume on Saudi-Iranian relations which covers the period, 1932-1982, beginning with the creation of the Kingdom of Saudi Arabia and continuing through the first years of the republican regime in Iran. This second volume covers the period 1982-1997.

The book is not politically motivated nor intended as a polemic to defend or justify Saudi policies or to attack on Iranian policies. Nevertheless, the author does present a definite point of view. His thesis is that although Saudi-Iranian relations have had their ups and downs since the Iranian revolution in 1979, the Kingdom always sought to maintain as cordial relations with Iran as possible, while Iran vacillated between periods of tension and coexistence; second, that while Iran saw itself in competition with Saudi Arabia for spiritual leadership of the Muslim world, Saudi Arabia did not see such competition as either in its interests or in the interests of the Muslim world; and third, that independent of its aspirations in the Muslim world, Iran sought to increase its political and economic influence throughout the Gulf, Near East and Africa as well, whereas Saudi aspirations were more narrowly focused on the welfare of Arab and Muslim societies, economic aid, and security.

Dr. Badeeb makes a good case for his thesis, particularly given the difficulties in obtaining primary source documentation for such a relatively recent period. Due to the sensitivities inherent in regional foreign policies in the Gulf, however, there are bound to be strong differences of opinion. That, however, does not at all detract from the value of the book. Perhaps its greatest value, particularly for the Western reader, is its authenticity. As he himself is the product of a regional Islamic culture, there is no occasion for the author to interpolate motives to foreign cultural perceptions or to reflect foreign political agendas in analyzing the events and situations he discusses. He is expressing his views on the basis of the societal perceptions of one of two players, Saudi Arabia. This is history through the lenses of one of the countries who made it.

David E. Long
Burke, Virginia

INTRODUCTION

This is my second book on contemporary Saudi-Iranian relations. The first book covered the years, 1932-1982, from the establishment of the creation of the Kingdom of Saudi Arabia to the establishment of the radical republican regime in Iran following the revolution of 1979. To remind the reader of what was covered in the first book, I wrote a chapter that deals with the historical evolution of relations between the two countries. Then, I focus on the current political relationship between the two countries. The third chapter discusses Saudi and Iranian ties with the Muslim World and the Arabian/Persian Arab Gulf States. The fourth chapter deals with the Saudi-Iranian relations with the Western World. A final chapter is dedicated to the future aspect of the relationship between the two countries.

The historical chapter looks at the period 1925-1932 --before the two countries formalized bilateral relations. King Abd Al-Aziz was in the last stages of unifying the modern Kingdom of Saudi Arabia, and Reza Pahlavi was seeking to create a modern state in what was then Persia. Though both leaders were primarily concerned with domestic issues, their proximity to each other across the Gulf set the stage for an increasingly important bilateral relationship. Using the evolution of the two countries into modern states and the development of their political system as points of comparison, I then look in more depth at Saudi-Iranian economic, religious, and military relations.

In the fifty years covered by my first book, both Saudi Arabia and Iran emerged from weak, regional states in a world dominated by Western imperial powers to become major international actors, themselves, largely due to the strategic and economic importance of their oil reserves. The importance of the present book, therefore, lies in its coverage of an existing bilateral relationship between these two major Muslim and Gulf States, and how it impacts on the politics and economics, not just of the Gulf region and the Arab World, but also on that of the Muslim World and the industrial countries of the West.

In this book, I argue that although Saudi Arabia has always tried its best to maintain as cordial relations with Iran as possible, Saudi-Iranian relations since the Iranian revolution have gone up and down, sometimes cooperative and sometimes confrontational. Due to the presence of the radical group that has ruled Iran since the revolution, it has been especially difficult to maintain good relations. On the Iranian side, there have been several attempts by more moderate elements to improve relations with Saudi Arabia, including an exchange of letters between His Majesty the Custodian of the two Holy Mosques and President Rafsanjani of Iran. However, all efforts were foiled by the radicals' stand. Unfortunately, the radicals still have the upper hand in Iran.

The strained relations with Saudi Arabia created by the radical Iranian political leaders have had a negative impact on the entire Muslim World, as both countries have pursued very different Islamic policies. Iran sees itself as the leader of Islamic revolution, which it seeks to spread that throughout the Muslim World. Saudi Arabia's Islamic policies, on the other hand, are aimed not at gaining political influence in the Muslim World but at preserving the faith. While Iran sees itself in competition with Saudi Arabia for leadership of the Muslim World, Saudi Arabia sees itself, as the custodian of the Muslim holy places, two Holy Mosques in Makkah and Al-Madinah. She does not seek to compete with any body, or seek political influence, but rather to preserve and strengthen Islam throughout the Islamic World.

In the Arab World, Saudi Arabia has tried to play a conciliating role, while Iran has tried to set Arab against Arab, supporting dissident Islamist groups in Sudan, Algeria, Egypt and elsewhere. In the Gulf, it is difficult to tell where Iran's revolutionary policy toward neighboring Arab States stops and where its Persian nationalistic policy begins. Many of its jingoistic policies in the Gulf are virtually indistinguishable from the Shah's policies of seeking Iranian hegemony in the Gulf region.

Saudi Arabia, on the other hand, has been reactive rather than proactive in the region, basically seeking peaceful coexistence with all Arab Gulf countries. This has mainly been done through the creation of the Gulf Cooperation Council in 1981, and its respective organizations.

Relations with the Western World also present a strong contrast. Iran views the West primarily as adversaries to its revolutionary policies, particularly the United States, which it castigates as the 'Great Satan'. The only motivation Iran seems to have in normalizing relations with the West is for what economic and political benefits it can thereby extract, not for what it can bring to the relationship. Saudi Arabia, on the other hand, sees the Western countries as partners in maintaining regional security, as well as major trading partners for oil, and as a major source of technology to improve the lives of its citizens.

In looking at future prospects for Saudi-Iranian relations, the chief variable will be Iran; Saudi Arabia has been constant in its efforts to create and maintain amicable if not warm relations with Iran, but to no avail. For example, in 1993 it sought to promote better political relations by sending a new ambassador to Tehran. The new ambassador carried a message to the President of Iran from His Majesty the Custodian of the Two Holy Mosques expressing his wishes for a new chapter in relations between the two countries. But again, the overture was rebuffed by the acts of the Iranian radicals and the relationship was put on hold.

For Iran, the variables lie in two areas - political and economic affairs and religious affairs. Current Iranian policies in both areas have failed to accomplish their objectives. This is largely due to the fact that, in policy terms, the two areas are combined and their revolutionary nature works at cross purposes with each other. The current economic crisis in Iran burdening the government is a good example. Because current Iranian government policy-making combines the two areas, the regime cannot meet the present goals and needs of the country.

Repressive domestic social policies in the name of 'revolutionary Islam' undermine economic development, and Iran's revolutionary religious policies abroad are not only disruptive throughout the Muslim World, but also discourage badly needed foreign investment to help improve economic and social conditions at home. Furthermore, Iran's nationalistic ambitions in the Gulf have strained relations with all its Gulf neighbors, including Saudi Arabia.

So long as Iran pursues an expansionist policy in the Gulf, the Kingdom of Saudi Arabia will remain uneasy about Iran's military build-up in the Strait of Hormuz and the disputed islands of Abu Musa, Greater and Lesser Tunbs. In fact, Iran has strengthened its forces in the Abu Musa Island recently and moved some of its troops and conventional arms into the island. Moreover, Iran's ambition to build up a nuclear power program has increased Saudi Arabia's concern. In reality, all these Iranian efforts have caused concern and worries in the Saudi eyes.

Another Saudi concern was Iran's support for terrorism. Its support for Hizballah in Lebanon, its support for Sudan, and its support for radical Shi'ites in the Gulf region, have all been matters of grave concern. As a state sponsoring terrorism, Iran has continued to support Hizballah in Lebanon, and finance its operations inside and outside Lebanon. She also has established good relations with Sudan, which became the 'kitchen' for terrorism, replacing Beirut. Moreover, she continued supporting the radical Shi'ites in the Gulf region particularly in Bahrain and Saudi Arabia.

All in all, the Saudi-Iranian relations have been unstable since 1982, having many ups and downs. Whereas some more moderate elements in Iran have tried to promote better relations between the two countries, radicals in the Iranian regime have succeeded in undermining all these efforts as the 'Will of Khomeini'. This will calls for discrediting Saudi Arabia in the Muslim World through sabotage, terrorism and propaganda. For example, Iran constantly calls for the 'internationalization' of the two holy mosques, i.e., the Haram Mosque in Makkah and the Prophet's Mosque in Al-Madinah, claiming that Saudi Arabia is not worthy to be entrusted with custodianship. The inference is that only Iran is worthy to lead the Muslim World through its brand of 'Islamic revolution'.

In sum, this book describes relations between Saudi Arabia and Iran from 1982 until 1997. It touches on important issues and analyzes the approach of the two countries toward those issues. I only hope that I was objective in my approach and have succeeded in my effort to discuss and analyze this bilateral relationship that is so important to stability in the Gulf and the entire Middle East region.

CHAPTER ONE

THE SAUDI-IRANIAN POLITICAL RELATIONS: 1982-1997

Introduction:

Soon after the Iranian revolution in 1979, Saudi Arabia recognized the new regime. Political relations between the two countries quickly deteriorated, however, reaching a new low following the outbreak of the Iran-Iraq war in 1981. From almost the start, the new Iranian regime appeared to go out of its way to antagonize its neighbors. Saudi Arabia responded with patience to Iranian antagonism and propaganda and tried its best to normalize political relations with Iran, but to no avail. The Kingdom was keen to establish a strong link with Iran as a fellow Islamic State, but the Iranian Mullahs, far from seeking cooperation in preserving the faith, insisted on subservience by all Muslims to their revolutionary political dogmas, and set out to export it throughout the Muslim World, beginning with the Arab Gulf States. For example, a month after the success of the Iranian revolution, Imam Khomeini met individually with a group of his followers and told them that they would rule the Arab Gulf States and divide the Gulf States among them.[1]

Efforts to export the Iranian revolution have extended far beyond the Gulf to the greater Arab World, and beyond that to the entire Islamic World. One of its primary instruments for accomplishing this has been terrorism. It has pursued a number of tactics to frighten the Arab Gulf States. Among the terrorist tactics supported by Iran have been attacks on Imams of Sunni mosques, such as occurred in Switzerland and Washington D.C., in the middle of the 1980s.[2]

Assassinating Iranian opposition leaders opposed to Khomeini has been another tactic adopted by Tehran -- in this case, not only to

1

spread the revolution abroad but also protect it at home. Supporting dissident Shi'a minorities in Arab Gulf States such as Bahrain and Saudi Arabia has been another tactic embraced by Tehran.

In Africa, the Iranian government has tried to gain political influence through financial support. For example, in the Ivory Coast, it has given financial assistance to Shi'a groups and built schools and Husayniyas (Shi'a religious complexes). In the Sudan, it has channeled financial aid to the government in support of a number of terrorist groups using the country for safe haven. It has also supported dissident Islamist groups in North Africa, particularly in Tunisia and Algeria. As a result, the Algerian government cut off its diplomatic relations with Iran in 1993 and closed the Iranian embassy in Algiers. Tunisia did not go to that extreme, but has been forced to monitor the movements of Iranian diplomats suspected of subversive activities. The Iranians have also been active in Morocco where they have antagonized the government by establishing secret contacts with the opposition groups there.

In Muslim States in South Asia, particularly in Pakistan, and in Southeast Asia, including Indonesia, Thailand, and Malaysia, the Iranian government has cooperated with dissident Shia as well as Sunni groups seeking to destabilize local governments. The Iranians also conducted subversive and terrorist activities in other Southeast Asian States. In Thailand, for example, they orchestrated an attack against three Saudi diplomats who were killed in front of their houses in 1989. In Malaysia, they started a campaign in 1993 to convert Sunni Muslims into Shi'ism, and to supporting dissident Muslim groups against the Malaysian government.

Saudi Arabia has been a principal target of Iranian revolutionary foreign policy, which it sees as a rival to leadership of the Muslim World. For example, since coming to power, the Iranian government has constantly called for the 'internationalization' of Makkah and Al-Madinah, charging that Saudi Arabia is not qualified to be the custodian of the two holy mosques located there -- the holiest sites in Islam. The Saudi responded by inviting all Muslims: 'Come and see with your own eyes the status of the two holy mosques'.

Since its revolution, Iran has also entered into a confrontation with the Western World, particularly the United States that, it calls 'The Great Satan'. On November 4, 1979, armed students attacked the

US embassy in Tehran and took over 100 hostages. This attack had personal approval of Ayatollah Imam Khomeini.[3] Tehran has also antagonized several European countries such as Germany and France when it was not seeking money from them.

Political Cooperation and Confrontation:

This chapter discusses the political relations between Saudi Arabia and Iran; we will then come back in other chapters to the issues of Iran's state-sponsored terrorism, its relations with the Islamic World, and its relations with the Western World.

In essence, the political relations between Saudi Arabia and Iran can be divided into two broad categories: political cooperation and political confrontation. Both categories have their own particular dynamics.

A: Political Cooperation:

The varying degrees of tension that have plagued Saudi-Iranian relations since the Iranian revolution of 1979 should not obscure the fact that political cooperation has occurred in a number of important areas. At the same time, it must be noted that while Saudi Arabia has strived for mutual cooperation, Iran has basically viewed the Kingdom as a rival and a competitor, even when Saudi Arabia was not seeking a competitive role. For the most part, therefore, where their policies have run parallel, it has been less the result of a conscious desire by Iran for political cooperation than of political coexistence out of mutual political self-interest.

The Saudi government, on the other hand, has always taken the position that it should encourage better relations with Iran wherever possible. Thus, in November 1979, Saudi Arabia announced that neither Iran, which was widely suspected of doing so, nor the United States, which Iran accused of doing so, were responsible for the forcible occupation of the holy mosque in Makkah that year.[4]

The following spring, Saudi Arabia gave its full support for the territorial integrity of Iran. On May 22, 1980, the conference of Islamic Foreign Ministers meeting in Islamabad adopted a resolution opposing any action against the sovereignty or territorial integrity of Iran, and warning against any imposition of economic sanctions against Iran.[5] During the meeting, the Saudi Foreign Minister voiced his country's strong support for the resolution.

Saudi support for Iranian sovereignty and territorial integrity has included opposition to economic sanctions against Iran, despite strong sentiments for such policies by some of its allies.[6] This support has included Saudi Arabia's willingness to support Iran against foreign intervention; and, second, it condemns military or economic aggression against the republic of Iran. In essence, Saudi support of Iranian sovereignty and territorial integrity has been full and comprehensive.

In the intervening years since the Iranian revolution, however, Saudi-Iranian cooperation was largely motivated by different reasons for each party. For example, since both countries espouse a revival of Islamic values throughout the Muslim World, one would think this would be an area in which they could cooperate. In fact, there has been far more confrontation than cooperation due to Iran's ambitions to be the sole spiritual leader of the Muslim World, wielding political as well as spiritual influence. These differences will be discussed more at length below.

It is interesting to note the degree to which Saudi and Iranian policies in regard to the Arab position in the Arab-Israeli conflict have coincided since the Iranian revolution despite major differences in perspectives. Saudi Arabia's opposition to Israel was based on justice - i.e. the Arab consensus that the creation of Israel was a grave injustice to the Palestinian people who were systematically denied self-determination; and Iran's opposition to Israel was for its own reasons and had little to do with the Arab consensus.

Nevertheless, following the Iranian revolution in 1979, the new regime severed its political and diplomatic relations with Israel. Thus, the policies of Iran and Saudi Arabia toward Israel overlapped to a great extent. Both Republican Iran and Saudi Arabia supported the Palestinian Liberation Organization (PLO) in its opposition to the Jewish State. Both countries condemned Israel for attacks against the PLO in July 1981, and appealed to the international community to condemn them. Saudi Arabia further offered a US$20 million indemnity to victims of the Israeli raids. The two countries also condemned the Israeli invasion of Lebanon in 1982; and both called for international condemnation of the invasion and for the immediate withdrawal of Israeli troops from Lebanon. They both called for

Israeli withdrawal from the Syrian Golan Heights and the return of that area to Syria. Republican Iran also supported the Arab Boycott of Israel. Iran continued to do business with companies on the boycott list, however, many of which had established business relations in Iran during the time of the Shah.[7] Saudi Arabia, by contrast, complied with the Arab boycott. For example, the Commerce Minister once warned the Toyota Motor Company that it would face retaliatory action under the Arab Boycott if it established business ties with the Ford Motor Company, which was on the boycott list at the time.

Saudi Arabia and Iran both broke relations with Egypt after it signed a peace agreement with Israel in 1979. However, the Kingdom severed relations with Egypt because President Sadat did not consult it or any other Arab State, and broke Arab consensus in signing the treaty, while Iran broke relations because it was essentially against any peaceful Middle East agreement with Israel. Iran's opposition to any Middle East peace constitutes a major area of difference with Saudi Arabia and will be discussed further below.

Iran's support of the Arab cause was also manifested following the Israeli invasion of Lebanon on June 6, 1982. It joined Saudi Arabia and other Arab States in condemning the invasion and calling on Israel to end its illegal occupation of Lebanon. The invasion was intended to force the removal of the PLO from Lebanon and put an end to PLO attacks on Israel from Lebanese territory. It succeeded in the former but not in the latter, in large part because its occupation of southern Lebanon was itself a major provocation to the PLO as well as the Lebanese. The underlying problem, however, was the denial of a whole people, the Palestinians, the right of self-determination; and that was the ultimate aim of the PLO.

In that regard, when the Saudi Foreign Minister, Prince Saud Al-Faysal, met with the US Secretary of State in Washington the following July, 19, he called upon the United States to recognize the PLO, based on the fact that it was de facto the sole representative of all Palestinians and spoke on their behalf in the international arena. Prince Saud's demand was met with a negative answer then, but the United States finally did recognize the PLO after the Oslo agreement between PLO Chairman Arafat and the Israelis in 1993, affirming that the only avenue to peace had to include the PLO.[8]

One of the most important instances in which Saudi and Iranian regional policies worked in parallel was Iraq's invasion of

Kuwait on August 2, 1990 and its occupation of Kuwait. The invasion was a surprise to virtually everyone in the area as well as outside, and the occupation was extremely brutal until Iraqi forces were driven out almost six months later by an international coalition of Arabs and Western powers.[9]

The Saudi government condemned the invasion and stood behind Kuwait from the start, giving safe haven to Kuwaiti refugees and allowing the Kingdom to be used as a staging area for the liberation of Kuwait in Desert Storm. Iran, like Saudi Arabia, supported the United Nations resolutions calling for the withdrawal of Iraqi troops from Kuwait, but stayed neutral in the fighting between Iraq and the international coalition that gathered in Saudi Arabia and other Arabian Gulf countries. In fact, Iran, which fought Iraq for eight years (1980-1988) with a minimum of outside assistance, initially opposed deploying Western troops in the region, although it supported the presence of Arab and Islamic forces.

Nevertheless, Iran stood silent over foreign troops until the war was over and Western, notably American troops were deployed in Saudi Arabia and the other Arab Gulf countries. Iran sees those troops as a threat to its own security, conveniently ignoring the fact that its own imperial designs on the Gulf constitute a major threat to regional troops that the foreign troops are there to help maintain.

In sum, Iran was supportive of the Gulf Arabs during the Iraqi invasion although its policies were to a degree self-serving. Iran was careful never to totally alienate Iraq; and if Saddam had appeared to be winning the confrontation, Iran could have quickly realigned its policies to conform to new realities. It also benefited by keeping the Iraqi aircraft that Iran had allowed to land in Iran for safe haven during the war. On the other hand, the Iranians were as happy as the Saudis and other members of the coalition that Saddam Hussein's forces were driven from Kuwait.

Iran must also be credited with not giving in to Saddam Hussein's obvious efforts to curry favor from the Iranian regime. To gain Iran's support for the occupation of Kuwait, Saddam announced his intention to free Iranian prisoners of war and to acknowledge Iranian sovereignty over virtually all territory Iraq took from Iran in their 1980-1988 war.[10] Saddam also failed in his efforts to use Iran's hatred of the United States and other European powers in the international coalition to induce it to join him against the coalition in the fighting. Iran condemned his actions and called for his withdrawal from Kuwait.

Closely related to the Iraqi invasion and occupation of Kuwait were Saudi and Iranian relations with the Iraqi opposition at the time. Both Saudi Arabia and Iran gave asylum to Iraqi refugees that escaped from Iraq in 1990. The opposition leaders condemned Saddam's invasion of Kuwait and his dictatorial rule of Iraq, and portrayed him as a brutal dictator and a cynical opportunist. However, the Iraqi opposition was divided into a number of camps with different views and ideas. Saudi Arabia listened sympathetically to the Iraqi opposition leaders and told them candidly that the Kingdom did not object to their establishing contacts with other powers in the region or with outside countries such as the United States or the United Kingdom. In this way, Saudi Arabia left the ground open for Iran to begin talking to the Iraqi opposition leaders and support their efforts against Saddam Hussein. Since then, Iraqi opposition leaders, along with their followers, have continued to visit Saudi Arabia and Iran, and many of them have taken political refuge in both countries, together with their families.[11]

Another related, though much older problem was the Kurdish problem. Saudi Arabia and Iran have supported the Iraqi Kurds in their struggle against the Iraqi regime. Many Iraqi Kurds have taken refuge in Iran; and there are also numbers of Kurds working in Saudi Arabia.

Both countries support the idea of establishing autonomous rule for the Kurdish people in northern Iraq. The Kurds are a separate people with a separate language and have generally been mistreated by the Iraqi regime in Baghdad.

At the same time, neither supports an independent Kurdish state. Iran might be tempted to see the breakup of present-day Iraq, its greatest regional military rival and perhaps an opportunity to force Iranian hegemony over the entire Gulf, but it also has a sizeable Kurdish minority of its own and would not want to see any precedent for Kurdish independence. Saudi Arabia has no hegemonic designs on its neighbors, but would also oppose such a shift in the geopolitics of the region. Creation of a Kurdish state would herald the collapse of Iraq which would be almost certain to undermine long-term stability in the area, not only through the loss of a major state actor, but also because there are large Kurdish minorities in Turkey as well as Iraq and Iran which might be encouraged to begin irridentist movements. Finally, the Saudi government recognizes the territorial integrity of all states in the Gulf region. The entire international community also shares this view. Thus, Saudi Arabia and Iran, in supporting Iraqi Kurdish autonomy but not independence, have parallel policies on the Iraqi Kurdish problem, but also policies that run parallel to those of the international community.

Looking beyond the Middle East and Gulf regions, Saudi Arabia and Iran also adopted parallel policies toward the Soviet Union, and after its collapse, toward Russia. Both countries condemned the Soviet Union for its military action in Afghanistan in the 1980s, and aided groups opposed to the communist puppet regime.[12] Afghanistan was a Muslim country, invaded by a communist state, in 1979, and from that perspective, the Saudi-Iranian position was very strong. The Saudi position was less compromising, however. In January 6, 1980, the Kingdom withdrew from the 1980 Olympic games in Moscow to protest the Soviet invasion of Afghanistan, and on April 7, 1981, severed diplomatic relations with the communist regime in Kabul that the Soviets had installed there. The Kingdom had no diplomatic ties with the Soviet Union. Iran did not cut its diplomatic relations with the Soviet Union, nor boycott the Olympic games.[13]

Following the Soviet withdrawal from Afghanistan in 1989, and particularly after the collapse of the Soviet Union in 1991, the two countries normalized relations with Moscow. Saudi Arabia, which had reestablished diplomatic relations with the Russians in September, 1990, agreed to send US$1 billion in emergency humanitarian aid including food, clothing and medicine to Russia by the end of 1991 in addition to the US$1.5 billion that it pledged earlier. On the Iranian side, President Hashemi Rafsanjani visited Russia and signed a number of agreements including a military one. Thus, in the space of two years, both Saudi Arabia and Iran established good relations with the new Republic of Russia.

Both states also established diplomatic relations with newly independent Muslim States of Central Asia. There, however, Iran adopted a far more confrontational attitude toward the Kingdom, as we shall see below.

Another important international issue on which Saudi Arabia and Iran saw eye to eye was the fate of Bosnia-Herzegovina. This newly established Muslim State which was created after the fragmentation of Yugoslavia in 1992, was almost immediately subjected to large-scale genocide by minority Bosnian Serbs, armed and equipped by the neighboring state of Serbia in what they called ethnic cleansing. Both Saudi Arabia and Iran considered the Serbian war against the Muslims of Bosnia-Herzegovina as an attack against all Muslims of the world. Since the fighting broke out in 1992, the two countries have supported Bosnia in all the international organizations and have extended political, economic, moral, and military assistance. Saudi Arabia extended financial support, food, and medicines; and Iran, despite an international embargo on arms shipments to either side, extended its military support to Bosnia. In both cases, their goals were the same, to see the survival of a newly independent Muslim state against ethnic cleansing by the Serbs.

When the new Iranian regime came to power in 1979, Saudi Arabia sought closer economic ties with it, believing that economic cooperation could lead to greater political cooperation. Thus, Iran and Saudi Arabia have maintained their trade relations and sought to promote them. However, trade between the two countries has declined. In the past, Saudi Arabia used to import quantities of Iranian carpets, pistachios, saffron, and caviar, but nowadays these Iranian imports are rarely found in that market.[14] By contrast, Iranian trade with other Gulf Arab States has increased, and Iranian commodity imports reach the shores of the Gulf Arab States on a daily basis.

More importantly, there has also been a degree of cooperation on oil policies, even though Saudi Arabia has long been a price moderate and Iran a price hawk. On March 27, 1979, just after the Iranian revolution, Saudi Arabia, in an effort to promote cooperation, supported the Iranian position at an Organization of Petroleum Exporting Countries (OPEC) oil Ministers' meeting in Geneva, Switzerland, calling for a 9 percent raise in oil prices, despite the long-standing Saudi policy of price moderation.[15]

Subsequently, however, the two countries failed to agree on common positions on prices and production rates at OPEC meetings in Geneva and London, where Iran was not willing to compromise its position as a quid pro quo to Saudi Arabia. On November 11, 1986, for example, the Custodian of the Two Holy Mosques, King Fahd, sent a message to Iranian President Ali Khameini expressing his country's desire for greater cooperation with Iran on OPEC matters. He proposed the reduction of OPEC production from the 28 billion barrels per day (bpd) benchmark crude to 18 billion bpd as a means of stabilizing prices. The Iranian President said that Iran would study the matter, but two days later, on November 13, 1986, the Iranian oil Minister announced that Iran would consider it only as a temporary measure, implying it did not want to lower its production. The Saudis considered this to be a rejection of their proposal and an indication that Iran intended to maintain high production regardless of its effect on prices. Since then, however, the two sides have agreed on a number of meetings on the policies of OPEC and have coordinated their efforts.

Despite the fact that the two countries continued to differ over oil prices and production rates, they still managed to maintain fairly good relations inside OPEC. The new Iranian regime came to power toward the end of the oil boom of the 1970s and early 1980s, which saw oil prices rise from US$2 per barrel to US$35 per barrel, briefly reaching US$42 per barrel at one point. Saudi Arabia opposed a rapid rise in oil prices, while the new regime, like its predecessor, pushed for as high prices as possible. Nonetheless, the two countries came to the conclusion that it was in their mutual interests to cooperate within OPEC to maintain a stable international oil market.

Whatever their other differences, the two countries have also always cooperated in keeping the Gulf open to crude oil shipments. Despite Iranian threats from time to time to close the Straight of Hormuz at the mouth of the Gulf to all shipping, Iran has not tried to do so and oil shipments continue to flow smoothly from the Gulf to world markets. For example, on April 27, 1980, Iran threatened to use military force to close the straight of Hormuz if the United States moved against it. Although this threat was mostly blustering, the US presence in Gulf has in fact caused a lot of concern to the Iranian regime. It has argued that the Gulf countries have the capability and willingness to protect the Gulf and defend themselves against any foreign attack. While this argument conveniently ignores threats from within the Gulf itself, there are many on the Arab side of the Gulf who also feel that Gulf security should be a Gulf responsibility. In any event, on the subject of oil policies and the unimpeded flow of oil through the Gulf, Iran and Saudi Arabia have exchanged letters in which they reached the conclusion that their cooperation in maintaining a stable oil market was a vital necessity to both countries, and indeed to the entire world.[16]

In sum, there is a far greater confluence of interests between

Saudi Arabia and Iran than is commonly realized. Where they have parallel interests and can agree on political issues, they have the ability to affect regional politics in a very positive way. Unfortunately, there are many areas where they cannot cooperate.

B: Political Confrontation:

Like the regimes of France and the United States, both the Saudi and Iranian regimes were born in revolution; unlike them, however, the Saudi revolution was an Islamic one -- its founder, Shaykh Mohammad ibn Abd Al-Wahhab sought to purify the Islamic World of the secular heresies that had crept into it over the centuries. Wahhabism, as this puritan revival movement became known in the West, also predated the American and French revolutions, having been established in the mid-eighteenth century. An early follower of the movement was Mohammad ibn Saud, the founder of the Saudi royal house, and it has been the basis of the Saudi political system ever since.

For the next two and one-quarter centuries, the Saudi regime stood almost alone among Islamic governments in seeking to purify the religion. Then, in 1979, an Islamic revolution occurred in Iran. Unlike the Wahhabi doctrine of Tawhid (strict monotheism), however, which sought to root out innovation, the Iranian revolution was based on a new, Shi'a interpretation of Islamic political theory of the Ayatollah Khomeini: Velayat-e-Fagih (Rule by Scholars of Islamic Jurisprudence). It said basically that the ultimate governing authority in an Islamic political system should be Islamic scholars, and while there were more learned and prestigious Ayatollahs in Iran at the time, Khomeini obviously considered himself the ultimate authority.

Saudi Arabia welcomed the creation of a brother Islamic regime in Iran and sought to establish cordial relations with it and avoid some of the confrontations over territory and other matters that existed during the time of the Shah. From its coming into power, however, the Iranian regime saw Saudi Arabia as a rival, not a friend, and adopted policies antagonistic toward it. The source of the antagonism was not because Saudi Arabia was godless or secular, but just the opposite, because it saw the Saudi vision of an Islamic society as a rival to its own vision which it intended to spread throughout the Islamic World under Iranian spiritual if not political hegemony.
The first challenge from Iran to Saudi Arabia over Islamic

policies was the call for the 'internationalization' of Makkah and Al-Madinah, sites of the two holiest places in Islam (translated in Arabic as Haramayn)-- the Haram Mosque in Makkah and the Prophet's Mosque in Al-Madinah. The Iranians claimed that Saudi Arabia did not deserve to be custodians of the two holy places, which they neglected and did not take adequate care of, and that an international Muslim World Committee should be established to take care of them. The political motivation behind these charges was Iran's ambition to be the leader of the Muslim World, and it saw Saudi Arabia's guardianship of the holy places as a major challenge to that ambition.

Saudi Arabia has condemned Iran for such patently false allegations. Once a year, the Kingdom administers the Hajj or Great Pilgrimage in which about one and one half million Muslims travel to Saudi Arabia from all over the world to visit the holy places in Makkah and al-Madinah; and in addition, thousands of Muslims travel to Makkah to perform the Little Pilgrimage, or Umrah during the rest of the year.[17] Moreover, in the past 35 years, Saudi Arabia has totally renovated the two holy mosques, enlarging them to accommodate the great crowds that now visit annually, and equipping them with the latest technological advances available on the market. In the process, Saudi Arabia has spent SR (Saudi Riyals) 70 billion, the equivalent of US$19 billion. The Saudi response to Iranian allegations of inviting all Muslims to come and see the status of the two holy mosques with their own eyes is justified in the millions of Muslims who visit the holy places each year and come away with their faith strengthened from the wonderful experience.

The second confrontation arose over Iran's ambitions to dominate the Gulf region. This confrontation is based in part on a clash of Arab and Persian nationalism, exemplified by the name of the Gulf itself. The Arabs have always called it the Arabian Gulf while the Iranians insist it is the Persian Gulf. Persian imperial ambitions, however, go far back in history and were even evident under the Shah. No sooner had the British announced in 1968 that they intended to end their protective status in the Gulf by 1971 than the Shah began to press a claim to Iranian sovereignty over Bahrain and three small islands in the Gulf -- Greater Tunb and Lesser Tunb, belonging to Ras Al-Khaymah, and Abu Musa, belonging to Sharjah.[18]

The Shah agreed to a plebiscite in Bahrain administered by the United Nations in which the Bahraini people chose independence. Following that setback, he invaded the Tunbs and Abu Musa but then signed an agreement with the Amirs of Ras Al-Khaymah and Sharjah to share the Islands for twenty years. After the twenty years expired, another agreement was to be signed by all parties to continue the sharing of the Islands or to return them to their original owners.

When the agreement expired in 1991, the United Arab Emirates (UAE), on behalf of Sharjah and Ras Al-Khaimah, which are now members of the UAE, demanded the return of the Islands to the custody of the Emirates. Iran refused to return them claiming that they were Iranian, and to strengthen their position, increased their military presence on the Islands.

The UAE is seeking a peaceful solution to this crisis, and has offered to refer the case to the International Court of Justice (ICJ) in Hague for arbitration. Iran has not agreed, and given the dubious nature of its claim, is not likely to do so. The Iranian government appears far more interested in keeping the issue alive in order to use it as a pressure point for future relations with the UAE.[19]

A third confrontation, which is really an extension of the first one mentioned above, results from Iran's ambition to spread its Islamic revolution to the entire Muslim World. We will talk about this topic in length in chapter two. This ambition, based on a combination of religious and imperial Persian motivations, affects Saudi-Iranian political relations in two respects. First, Iranian foreign policy is potentially highly destabilizing politically; it concentrates far more on spreading revolution than spreading Islam. Second, because Iran sees Saudi Arabia a rival for leadership over the entire Muslim World, much of its policy of spreading its revolution is focused against Saudi Arabia.

Many aspects of Iran's Islamic foreign policies are admirable. It supports Muslim organizations and builds mosques, schools, hospitals, and Hussainiyahs (Shi'a religious centers) in many Muslim countries. At the same time, however, it uses these activities for its own political agenda -- to become the sole spiritual if not the political leader of all Muslims by spreading its brand of Islamic revolution throughout the Muslim World.

Originally Iran concentrated its efforts on radical Shi'a groups, for example by giving scholarships to young Shi'a Muslims to study in Iran where they would be given training in both Shi'a principles and revolutionary tactics. However, when the regime saw that the Iranian revolution had little appeal among Sunni Muslims who comprise great majority of all Muslims, it broadened its support to include all radical Muslim groups, Shi'a or Sunni alike. Thus, Iran tried to infiltrate many Muslim religious organization and associations to gain political influence over them, and to give financial, logistical and training support to radical anti-government Muslim political groups, particularly in countries that the regime was considered a threat to its ambitions. It has been particularly active in supporting radical Shi'a groups such as Hizballah in Lebanon and other groups in Bahrain, Iraq, Afghanistan and in Muslim central Asia; but it has also supported revolutionary Sunni groups, much of it channeled through the Sudan. It has been less successful with Sunnis, however, witnessed by rebuffs from the Muslim Brotherhood and the Gama'at Islamiya in Egypt.

In the face of these activities, Saudi Arabia felt that it could not be an idle bystander. It therefore launched a campaign to lessen destabilizing Iranian political influence. First, it increased its own support of Islamic organizations in the Islamic World. Second, it sought to return a focus on the religion rather than on politics by distributing millions of copies of the Holy Qur'an and other religious materials to Muslim countries. The Custodian of the Two Holy Mosques Establishment for Printing the Holy Qur'an publishes copies of the holy book. Third, it continued building mosques and schools for Muslims all over the Islamic World. Fourth, it expanded its programs for sending Islamic teachers and preachers to the Islamic communities worldwide.

After 1991, a major focus of Iranian policy was to establish political influence in the newly independent Muslim States of former Soviet central Asia. They are: Azerbaijan, Turkmenistan, Uzbekistan, Tajikistan, Kazakhstan, and Kirghizstan. Iran quickly established diplomatic relations and financial aid programs with these countries. It also began sending Islamic teachers and preachers to them, and offering scholarships to their students.

Iran also sought to establish economic and commercial relations with the six Muslim central Asian countries, to provide additional markets for its products and seek closer policy coordination with those of them that produce oil. In 1992, Iran expanded the Central Economic Organization (ECO), which it established in 1985 with Turkey and Pakistan, to include the six central Asian countries plus Afghanistan.

Concerned that Iran's missionaries were more intent on

political agitation, Saudi Arabia sent its own Islamic preachers and teachers to the former Soviet republics, but to preach and teach and not stir up the population.[20]   It also quickly established political and economic relations as well and received central Asian presidents and political, economic and religious delegations in Riyadh. The Kingdom also extended financial assistance, and financed the renovation and construction of mosques, schools and hospitals.

Thus, despite the fact that Saudi Arabia had no political ambitions in the new Muslim republics of central Asia, it found itself drawn into a rivalry with Iran that serves neither their interests nor those of the republics. From the Saudi perspective, it would be better for the republics to look to Turkey than Iran as they seek to broaden their contacts with the Muslim World and at the same time seek assistance in the development process. In fact, those countries prefer a Turkish relationship.

As we have seen, a major Iranian tactic in exporting its revolution has been its support of terrorism.   For Saudi Arabia, terrorism is an immoral act of cowardice, which it categorically condemns.   Iran, on the other hand, while it publicly condemns terrorism, condones it in its every action as the greatest supporter of terrorism since the collapse of the Soviet Union.   It has provided financial and logistical assistance and training to terrorist groups throughout the Muslim World and in the West, either directly or through surrogates like the Sudan.   Radical Islamic organizations supported by Iran include Hamas in Palestine, Hizballah in Lebanon, the Front for Islamic Salvation (FIS) in Algeria, the Bahraini Liberation Movement (BLM), and many of the leading Egyptian terrorist organizations.   It has also facilitated networking by many radical Arab volunteers who fought against the Communists in Afghanistan, and who have organized a nucleus of terrorist groups. Many of these terrorist groups and individuals are located in the Sudan, which has become a major conduit for Iranian financial support.

Iran's support of terrorism extends beyond simply exporting its Islamic revolution, however; it supports radicalism in general. Thus, radicalism and revolution are two of Iran's preferred policy tools for changing not only the Islamic World, but the Arab World as well. For example, in addition to Hamas, Iran supports about ten radical, secular Palestinian groups implacably opposed to any Middle East peace settlement, including the Abu Nidal Organization (ANO), George Habash's Popular Front for the Liberation of Palestine (PFLP), Ahmed Jibril's PFLP General Command, Naif Hawatmah's Democratic Front for the Liberation of Palestine.[21] Habash himself is not even a Muslim but a Greek Orthodox Christian.

Saudi Arabia, by contrast, deplores radicalism. It has adopted a policy of not interfering in the internal affairs of other countries, and expects as a quid pro quo for other countries not to interfere in its internal affairs. And no matter how worthwhile or not a radical organization's political goals might be, seeking to attain them by the use of terrorism and violence against innocent, defenseless civilians cannot be justified.

There are two other highly confrontational issues in Saudi-Iranian political issues that are basically military in nature. One has to do with Iran's acquiring weapons of mass destruction (WMD), nuclear, biological and chemical weapons; and the second has to do with the maintaining of security in the Gulf region.

On the issue of proliferation, Iran, in contradictory claims asserts, first that it is not acquiring WMD at all, and second, that it is developing nuclear capabilities solely for peaceful purposes. This claim simply does not conform to the facts. Iran's signing of military agreements with the Peoples Republic of China, and North Korea make virtually no sense without its seeking to acquire weapons of mass destruction. Second, Iran claims that it must acquire all weapons it can for its own self-defense. It is true that the protracted Iran-Iraq war and gross mismanagement of its own defense establishment in the early years of the revolution greatly reduced Iran's ability to defend itself and that it has a legitimate need to restore its military capabilities. At the same time, however, there is simply no justification, least of all on defensive grounds, to acquire nuclear, biological and chemical weapons that can wipe out millions of innocent civilians.

The second issue is Gulf security. It was mentioned above that both Saudi Arabia and Iran have major interests in preventing military hostilities from breaking out in the Gulf region. The Gulf itself is a major route not only for oil exports, but also for crucial imports. Hostilities that threaten closure of the Gulf sea lanes would threaten the economies of both countries. Therefore, they both are keen to keep the Gulf open and the region stable. However, each country has it's own interpretation of what regional stability is. The Iranians give a narrow interpretation of Gulf security as preventing military actions that could interdict oil shipments. This has not stopped it, however, from supporting dissident political groups in the Arab Gulf States, and trying to use its military power to intimidate the Gulf Arabs into making political concessions on such issues as sovereignty over the Gulf Islands of Greater and Lesser Tunb and Abu Musa. Saudi Arabia, on the other hand, believes that true Gulf security must include political stability and not interfering with the internal affairs of its neighbors.

The greatest difference in outlook on Gulf security between Saudi Arabia and Iran, however, has to do with the continued presence of foreign, notably US, British, French and other Arab troops in the Gulf since their participation in Desert Storm in 1991 to help liberate Kuwait. Iran rejects the foreign military presence, claiming that it is against its interests in the region, and more particularly, is a hostile gesture against Iran. It charges that US troops in the Gulf are a direct threat against Iran. The Iranian government claims that Gulf security should be the sole responsibility of the Gulf states themselves, including Iran.

Iran asserts that strengthening its own armed forces near the Gulf and building up its military power on the disputed islands it claims is in order to insure Gulf security. For example, in 1996, it adopted a naval expansion program, which it called 'the week for holy defense'. This program aims at rebuilding Iranian naval forces and equipping them the latest and most advanced weapons. To enhance naval capabilities, the main naval elements that are under the command of the army conduct more than fifty maneuvers a year with naval units under the Revolutionary Guard. Iran also conducts annual 'Badr' naval exercises in the waters of the Gulf.[22]

Saudi Arabia agrees in principle that Gulf security is primarily the responsibility of the Gulf States, and it also does not allow the deployment of combat troops in the Kingdom. Nevertheless, it believes the stabilizing influence of coalition forces in the Gulf is an important aid to Gulf security. From the Saudi perspective, the foreign military presence in the Gulf is to help maintain peace, to protect the Gulf States from external attack and military adventurism, and to maintain freedom of the seas to protect the flow of oil from the Gulf countries - 20 percent of the world's total exports. The presence of coalition forces is both in their interests and those of the Gulf States.

Unfortunately, Iran itself, because of its aggressive political and military behavior toward the Arab Gulf States, must be considered along with Iraq as the greatest current threat to Gulf security and regional stability. All the Gulf States of the Arabian Peninsula have expressed the desire for good relations with Iran, and there is no regional threat to Iran other than Iraq to justify its military build up in the lower Gulf. The coalition forces and the United Nations have moved to keep the Iraqi and Iranian threats in check, and when those threats no longer exist, their presence will no longer be necessary.

We discussed above how Iran and Saudi Arabia's policies toward the Arab-Israeli problem overlap considerably. At the same time, their positions on the Arab-Israeli peace process are diametrically opposed. Saudi Arabia long supported an Arab-Israeli peace provided it was based on mutual justice, including exercise of the right of self-determination by the Palestinian people. Then Crown Prince Fahd enunciated the Saudi position in his eight-point plan presented to the Arab Summit Conference in Fez, Morocco On August 8, 1981. The points were:[23]

(1) Israeli withdrawal from all Arab territories occupied after 1967, including occupied East Jerusalem.
(2) The removal of Israeli settlements established on Arabs lands since 1967.
(3) The guarantee of freedom of worship and religious rights for all religions in the holy places of Jerusalem.
(4) Affirmation of the rights of the Palestinian people to return to their homes and compensation for those who decide not to do so.
(5) A transitional United Nations mandate over the West Bank and the Gaza strip for not more than a few months.
(6) The establishment of an independent Palestinian state with Jerusalem as its capital.
(7) The guarantee of the right of the Palestinian people to live in peace.
(8) The right of the states in the region to live in peace.[24]

The plan was first rejected in the conference, and Crown Prince Fahd had to withdraw it. The rejection came primarily from Syria, Iraq and the PLO. However, the British Foreign Secretary, Lord Carrington, expressed full support for the Saudi peace plan on

November 5, 1981. But in the next conference, which was held also in Morocco, in 1982, all members of the Arab League including the Palestinian Liberation Organization accepted it.

For Iran, however, it is not a matter of securing a just peace for the Palestinian people. Iran is essentially opposed to the peace process altogether. It considers Israel as an enemy of all Arabs and Muslims and as the occupier of Arab and Islamic land. It wants to destroy Israel entirely, and create instead an Islamic State built on the Iranian model and under its tutelage. It is within this perspective that Iran supports Hamas, which is fighting the Israelis from inside, and Hizballah, which is fighting the Israelis from Lebanon.

All in all, we have described in this chapter a broad picture of the political relations between Saudi Arabia and Iran. The examination of facts has touched on the ups and downs in their bilateral relationship. It also has discussed their relations with third parties, and how those relationships affect Saudi-Iranian bilateral relationship. Probably the main lesson to be learned, however, is that no matter how confrontational their relations, there are sufficient mutual interests for the two countries to live together in peace and harmony if Iran so chooses.

FOOTNOTES

(1) Personal papers.
(2) Ibid.
(3) 'Middle East Journal', Washington, D.C., 1970-1995, on November 4,1979.
(4) On November 22, 1979, Muslim gunmen seized the Grand mosque in Makkah and took hostages.
(5) Middle East journal, Washington, D.C. 1970-1995.
(6) On April 27, 1980, the United States breaks diplomatic relations with Iran, and urges its allies to take strong economic and political measures against it.
(7) The two countries wanted to avoid any Arab criticism of the communiqué. Therefore, they did not mention their economic relations in it. Both the Shah and King Saud knew the bad consequences of mentioning the economic relations.
(8) 'Global Arabic Encyclopedia', Encyclopedia Works Publishing & Distribution, Riyadh, Kingdom of Saudi Arabia, 1996, PP. 261-263.
(9) His majesty King Fahd Ibn Abd Al-Aziz spoke on TV about the reasons that led Saudi Arabia to help Iraq. That was in August 1990, after the Iraqi invasion of Kuwait. He said that Saudi Arabia has supported Iraq to avoid an Iranian victory over it.
(10) 'The New York Times', Thursday, January 31, 1991.
(11) The Iraqi opposition was so divided. It has different approaches to the Iraqi issue. They take refuge in the United Kingdom, particularly in London, in the United States of America, in Saudi Arabia, in Jordan, and in Iran.
(12) On December 22,1979, the Soviet Union started airlifting into Kabul.
(13) Saudi Arabia had no diplomatic or political relations with the Soviet Union.
(14) Iranian trade with the Gulf countries has tripled between 1964 and 1966, including Saudi Arabia. The Iranian exports to Saudi Arabia were estimated at IR 10,057 million (IR=US$ 60).
(15) 'Middle East Journal', Washington, D.C., 1970-1995, on March 27, 1979.

(16) Before the discovery of oil on the Saudi soil in 1938, King Abd Al-Aziz did not believe in borderlines. He considers the Arabian Peninsula, including the Gulf States, as one part.

(17) There are more than one million people who come for Umrah from all over the Islamic World, particularly in the month of Ramadan. Another one million people come during Hajj time every year, plus one million from inside the Kingdom.

(18) In 1968, Shah Mohammad Reza Pahlavi visited Saudi Arabia. He met with King Faisal Ibn Abd Al-Aziz. The King persuaded the Shah to abandon his claim and allow the United Nations to conduct its investigation. The UN has conducted its investigation and Bahrain became an independent state.

(19) See Dr. Saeed Mohammad Badeeb, 'Saudi-Iranian Relation (1932-1982)', Center for Arab and Iranian Studies and Echoes, 1993, p.121.

(20) 'The New York Times', Wednesday, October 9,1991.

(21) The ten Israeli opposition groups take to Syria as a safe haven. They meet and operate from Syria. They are entirely supported by Syria, Iran, and Libya.

(22) Tehran Broadcasting, 09/23/1996.

(23) 'Middle East Journal', Washington, D.C., August 8, 1981.

(24) Richard M. Preece, 'At The Saudi Peace Proposals, at Washington D.C'., Congressional Research Service, Library of Congress, 24 November, 1981, p.4.

CHAPTER TWO

SAUDI IRANIAN RELATIONS AND THE ISLAMIC WORLD

The impact of Saudi-Iranian relations on the greater Islamic World and of Islamic World politics on Saudi-Iranian relations is a fascinating subject. Both countries place a high priority on their Islamic foreign policies and go to great lengths to promote good relations with all Muslim communities. However, there are major differences in their approaches to Islamic World politics. Iranian Islamic foreign policy is self-avowedly revolutionary in nature. As a result of its militant interpretation of Islamic political obligations, it does not hesitate to interfere in the internal political affairs of other Islamic States whose politics it does not agree with, not only through propaganda attacks but also through the use of force by supporting local terrorist and guerrilla groups. Even its diplomats are heavily engaged in spreading the revolution. The use of violence has not achieved the Iranian objective to spread its revolution and to become the leading power in the Muslim World. On the contrary, it has gained for Iran many enemies. In the long run, violence begets only violence.

There is a complicating factor, however. Largely as a result of its revolutionary foreign policies, particularly its worldwide support for Islamist terrorism, Iran has become very isolated in world affairs. Economic sanctions and embargoes have greatly undermined its already faltering economy. Thus, breaking out of its isolation has become a major foreign policy imperative. Because this policy is totally incompatible with spreading the Islamic revolution, and because Iran in recent years is pursuing both policies at the same time, it is sometimes difficult to understand the seeming inconsistencies in its relations with other countries, particularly Muslim countries. Unfortunately for Iran, nobody has taken Iranian promises to moderate its foreign policies at face value and it has failed to break its isolation.

Saudi Arabia has a very different approach in its relations with other Islamic States through consultation and mutual consensus. In the words of King Fahd, "We do not interfere in anyone's affairs and do not want anyone to interfere in our affairs. We want to be friends within the limits of our Islamic faith".[1]

One of the most vivid examples of the differences between these two approaches toward Islamic World politics concerns Saudi and Iranian relations with the newly independent Islamic republics of Central Asia following the collapse of the Soviet Union. Iran has followed a very aggressive policy in Central Asia as it has tried to extend its political influence over these new states. In doing so, it has consistently viewed Saudi Arabia as a competitor and threat to its interests. The Saudis, by contrast, have not seen themselves in competition with Iran, nor have they sought political hegemony in this important part of the Muslim World. Rather, they have concentrated on extending aid and encouragement to the newly independent Islamic Republics of Central Asia as they begin the task of nation building and of restoring the Islamic values that were submerged during the period of atheistic Soviet domination.

The Islamic World is far larger than the casual observer might realize. It extends from the Atlantic Ocean in Africa to the Pacific Ocean in the Philippines, and northward to the Balkans in Central Europe as well as almost all of Central Asia. There are about one billion Muslims worldwide. In examining the implications on Saudi-Iranian relations of their contrasting approaches to the Islamic World, we will look in turn at the main sub-regions in which both Saudi Arabia and Iran are primarily engaged. We will begin with the Arab World. From there we will move to the South Asian countries and their relationship with Saudi Arabia and Iran, the countries of South East Asia next and then the countries of Central Asia. Finally, some mention will also be made of the Muslim countries of sub-Saharan Africa but as neither Saudi Arabia nor Iran is heavily engaged there, the impact of their policies on Saudi-Iranian relations is relatively small.

Before we begin, however, let us first discuss briefly the religious systems in each country, i.e. Saudi Arabia and Iran. Comparing and contrasting their different religious practices and histories can help in understanding the differences in their approaches to Islamic foreign policies.

The Saudi Religious System:

The population of Saudi Arabia is virtually entirely Muslim. About 90 percent of the population are Sunnis, or Orthodox Muslims, who comprise most of the world Muslim population, and about 10 percent are Shi'ites, or Heterodox Muslims. Saudi Arabia is more than an Islamic country, however; it is the cradle of Islam. It was in Makkah and Al-Madinah, in the Hijaz, now the country's Western Province, that the Prophet Mohammad, Peace Be Upon Him, brought Allah's revealed word, the Holy Quran, to the people.[2]

This Islamic heritage has had a profound impact on every aspect of Saudi life. It is impossible to separate one's personal and public life from the teachings of Islam. These teachings constitute the Shari'a, or Islamic law, and are literally the constitution of the country. The sources of the Holy Law are the Quran and the Sunna, the inspired traditions of the Prophet. They embody laws laid down by Allah on religious and worldly matters governing every field of human activity and worship. In brief, it is a comprehensive system for human life as well as for the requirements of the hereafter. To emphasize its Islamic heritage, the Kingdom has adopted as its flag a green field upon which are the words of the Shahadah, the Islamic declaration of faith, La ilaha illa Allah, wa Mohammadun rasulu Allah, There Is no god but Allah and Mohammad is the messenger of Allah.

Makkah and Al-Madinah, where the Prophet lived and preached, are considered the holiest sites in Islam and are visited by nearly two million of the faithful each year during the annual Hajj or Great Pilgrimage. One of the five pillars of the faith, the Hajj is required of all Muslims at least once in their lifetimes if they are financially and physically able to attend. Thousands more visit the two holy cities during the rest of the year to observe the Umrah, or Lesser Pilgrimage.

In Makkah is located the Haram Mosque, in the center of which is a simple stone structure covered by a gold and black velvet drape, the sacred Kabah. It is considered the geographical heart of Islam, toward which Muslims all over the world face five times a day in prayer. In Al-Madinah is found the Prophet's Mosque and is the site of his burial. So important are these holy cities to the Islamic World that King Fahd has taken the title, Khadim Al-Haramayn, or Custodian of the Two Holy Mosques. The advent of modern means of travel has necessitated expansion of the Haram and Prophet's Mosques to accommodate the millions of visitors each year, principally during the Hajj. The most recent expansion, carried out by King Fahd, was completed in 1994.[3]

There is a great deal of confusion among non-Muslims about what Saudi Muslims believe. Islam is essentially a system of laws, God's laws, and Sunni Islam recognizes four Madhhabs, or schools of Islamic jurisprudence: Hanafi, Maliki, Shafi'i and Hanbali. The official Saudi Madhhab is the Hanbali School, a very conservative school on social and family matters but liberal in other areas, notably in commercial affairs. A majority, though not all Saudi Sunni Muslims are Hanbalis, but the other Madhhabs are also recognized.

Most of the confusion arises over Saudi affiliation with Wahhabism. Wahhabism is not a school of jurisprudence, but rather a revival movement founded by Shaykh Mohammad Ibn Abd Al-Wahhab in the mid-eighteenth century. Although the Shaykh (his descendents have taken the surname, Al Al-Shaykh, or The House of the Shaykh, was a Hanbali, the revival movement is not limited to Hanbalis alone. It was conceived as an attempt to rid Islam of false religious practices that had arisen over the centuries and to return to the pure practices dictated by the Quran and the Sunna.

Mohammad Ibn Abd Al-Wahhab preached the doctrine of Tawhid, meaning strict monotheism, and his followers were known as Muwahideen, or Monotheists. The movement's detractors, however, called them Wahhabis, after the name of the founder, and the name stuck. Strict Muwahideen reject the name, Wahhabi, for its implication that Mohammad Ibn Abd Al-Wahhab and not Allah is the object of their worship. In any event, Mohammad Ibn Saud, ruler of a small central Arabian principality of Dariyah and the founder of the Saudi royal family, became an early supporter of the Shaykh, and the revival movement, and it has provided the Islamic ideological impetus for the Saudi State ever since.

The alliance of the religious reformer and the political leader proved irresistible, and by the turn of the nineteenth century, much of Arabia including Makkah and Al-Madinah were under Saudi control. The Ottoman Sultan, who was also recognized as the Caliph of all

Muslims and guardian of the two holy shrines, considered Saudi control of the holy cities to be a threat to his leadership and asked his wali (governor) in Egypt, Mohammad Ali, to send a military force to the Hijaz to regain control of the two holy cities. After fierce fighting, the two holy shrines were recaptured in 1816. Two years later, the Saudi capital at Dariyah was occupied by Egyptian-Ottoman troops.

This did not signal the end of Saudi rule, however. In 1824 the Sauds again seized control over Najd, as central Arabia is called, establishing their new capital at Riyadh. For the next 15 years, the dynasty experienced ups and downs, including a second Egyptian occupation, and regained full control in 1840. At the end of the century, they yet again lost power due to internecine power struggles to the rival House of Rashid from the northern principality of Hail. The last Saudi Amir, Abd Al-Rahman, fled to Kuwait.

His son, Abd Al-Aziz, known in the West as Ibn Saud, recaptured Riyadh in 1902, and after a quarter century of conflict, restored Saudi control over Najd with his tribal army of Muwahideen warriors. He subsequently organized them into an Islamic religious brotherhood called the 'Ikhwan,' which literally means ithe Brethren.[4]

Between 1924 and 1926, Abd Al-Aziz recaptured the Hijaz including the two holy cities of Makkah and Madinah, and took the title, King of the Hijaz and Sultan of Najd. In 1932, the country was named 'The Kingdom of Saudi Arabia'.

By history, tradition and faith, Islam is indelibly intertwined in the lives, society and politics of Saudi Arabia. Islam is the official religion of the country, the Holy Quran is its constitution, and Islamic law, the Shari'a, is the law of the land. Even its sense of time is Islamic. The Kingdom officially follows the Islamic Hegra calendar, based on the date of Prophet Mohammad's migration from Makkah to Al-Madinah. As for its history, Saudi Arabia and the Arabian Peninsula is the heart land of Islam. It is where Islam was born. From its land arose a military power that conquered half of the globe within one hundred years, including Persia. The leadership of the Kingdom and its population are proud of that history.

The Iranian Religious System:

Iran, or Persia as it was historically called, was converted to Islam in 634 AD during the time of Omar Ibn Al-Khattab whose armies conquered most of the Arab World including Damascus, Jerusalem, Egypt and Libya as well as Persia. Iran's rulers embraced Sunni Islam until the seventeenth century when the Safavid dynasty (1502-1736) established the Twelver branch of Shi'ism as the official state religion. Since then, Shi'ite doctrines have had a major influence on Persian thought, culture and politics and have become inextricably enmeshed with Persian/Iranian nationalism. Iran is the only country in the Muslim World where Shi'ite Islam is the official religion.

Shi'ites form a minority of Muslims worldwide, although in a few countries they actually constitute a majority, such as Iraq and Bahrain as well as Yemen where the ruling elite are predominantly Shi'ites of the Zayidi branch. Initially, the differences were primarily political rather than doctrinal or juridical and both follow the Shari'a, or Islamic law. But over time, doctrinal differences began to appear. Twelvers, the largest Shi'ite sect, believe that the twelfth Shi'ite Imam, or leader, did not die, but went into a state of occultation from which he will return at the end of history. He is therefore called the Hidden Imam. This messianic innovation adds a dimension of mysticism to the religion that many Sunnis believe is on the verge of heresy.

Because the Hidden Imam is still theoretically the head of state, the legitimacy of secular rulers in Shi'ite Persia and now Iran have historically been open to question, and many conservative Iranian clergy have claimed that the only function of temporal political leaders is to carry out the dictates of Islamic law as interpreted by the clergy. Ayatollah Khomeini took this a step farther in his revolutionary political theory, 'Velayat-e-Faqih' (the guardianship of the [Islamic] jurists, i.e. the Shi'ite clergy), which gave political supremacy to the Mullahs by virtue of their exclusive right to interpret the Holy law.

This power struggle between Shi'ite temporal and spiritual leaders has been a major element of Persian/Iranian history, with the clergy sometimes allying with secular leaders and sometimes opposing them. For example, Reza Khan Pahlavi, who seized power in 1921, and in 1925 ousted the last Qajar Shah and crowned himself as the Shah of Iran, would probably not have succeeded without the support of Mullahs and their blessing. But, the honeymoon did not last for long and a confrontation began between him and the Mullahs, when he attempted to limit their powers to religious endowments and education.

Reza Shah tried to turn Iran into a secular independent state, using as a model the Turkish system of Kamal Ataturk. He tried to exclude the Mullahs totally from political affairs, limiting their role to traditional religious affairs, education, and Islamic culture. He also tried to discourage the people from overt religious activities such as attending the Hajj, encouraging them instead to spend the money they would otherwise use for the pilgrimage to build up the economy of the country.

In 1941, Reza Shah was forced to abdicate in favor of his son Mohammad Reza Shah Pahlavi. After World War II, the new Shah had to cooperate with the Mullahs to beat the communists, whom he was able to defeat in 1954. But again, the honeymoon between the Shah and the Mullahs did not last long due to the Shah's alliance with the Western World, particularly the United States. Following in his father's footsteps, the Shah also cracked down on the political powers of the Mullahs.

During the energy crisis years of the 1970s, rapid modernization created many social dislocations; and taking advantage of them, the Mullahs' political activities resurfaced in 1977 and gained a wide range of public support.[5] On 16 January 1979, the Shah was forced into exile. Two weeks later, on February 1, a leading anti-government religious figure, Ayatollah Ruhollah Khomeini, returned to Tehran from exile and very quickly began the process of converting the country from a monarchy to a revolutionary republican theocracy. A new constitution, embodying elements of his doctrine of 'Velayat-e-Faqih', was adopted the following December, and he became the supreme religious guide of the country, in effect the head of state who ranked over the president.

The early years of the Republic were characterized by brutal excesses at home, and abroad the new regime attempted to impose its intolerant brand of revolution through the Muslim World. Seeing Saudi Arabia as a major threat to its ambition to be the leader of the Muslim World, Iran tried to undermine Saudi guardianship of the Holy places by fomenting riots at the Hajj, and undermining governmental authority by supporting subversive activities among the Saudi Shi'ite community. Both policies failed.

Since the death of Ayatollah Khomeini in 1989, Iran's subversive policies have moderated, but not its ambitions to be the leader of the Muslim World. The power of the extremist radical clergy in the government has made it impossible for all but the most modest overtures toward more moderate reform. There are still over one thousand Iranian Mullahs who oppose any peaceful overtures to mend the fences between Iran and the moderate Arab World including Saudi Arabia. They see their task as protecting the revolution and implementing what they believe was Khomeini's vision of a radical, revolutionary Muslim World, driving out all secular, Western political, economic and social influences, and radicalize the Arab World as well as the Islamic World.

The conduit for their influence is Ayatollah Ali Khamenei, successor to Khomeini as the spiritual leader of Iran. Moderating influences, which voice the sentiments of most of the Iranian people, sought their first, small successes under President Rafsanjani and more recently, President Mohammad Khatami. Even Khatami, however, known for his relatively more moderate views than the radical wing of the clergy, is severely limited in what he can do to cool the fires of extremism still seen in both Iranian domestic and foreign policies. In the meantime, the Iranian people must still wait for policies that will enable Iran to end its isolation and live peacefully with its neighbors. This cannot happen without a radical change in Iran and its institutions. Nevertheless, that change is coming even if no one can predict a precise date.

Saudi Arabia, Iran and the Arab World:

Saudi Arabia and Iran and their predecessor states have had religious relations with each other and the rest of the Arab World for centuries, due, in Saudi Arabia's case mainly to the Hajj, and in Iran's case, to its self-appointed role as defender of Shi'ite Muslims throughout the Arab World, and more recently, its ambitions to be the leading political power in the Middle East and entire Muslim World.

Saudi Arabia has a dual interest in the Arab World. It is a fellow Arab state, located in the heartland of the Arabs -- the Arabian Peninsula. Of equal importance, it is a fellow Muslim State, as stated above, and the heartland of Islam. After King Abd Al-Aziz reunified the Saudi Kingdom by the mid 1920s, he turned his attention beyond the Arabian Peninsula to the broader Arab World. It was still under colonial control of the West, and King Abd Al-Aziz struggled for its total independence, not thinking about individual borders. Until oil was discovered in commercial quantities in 1938, linking national economic well being forever with national territory, he considered the entire Arab World as one and believed that national borders were unnecessary.

King Abd Al-Aziz, as ruler of the only truly independent Arab state, championed Arab independence until it was fully realized. His successors were also strong supporters of Arab unity. For example, Saudi Arabia was a staunch supporter of the Algerians in their struggle for independence against the French, which they achieved in 1962.

Nevertheless, their greater concern was not secular Arab nationalism but Islamic unity in the Arab World in the face of secular and anti-Islamic threats. King Faysal summarized these threats as Zionism, colonialism and communism. He saw Zionism as an alien, expansionist, secular political ideology planted in the midst of the Muslim heartland, i.e. the Arab nation; colonialism was a threat because, by denying full freedom to the Arabs, encouraged radical, atheistic doctrines such as Arab socialism and communism among its disenfranchised citizens; and communism, the most atheistic doctrine of all and was thus the greatest threat of his time, not only to the Arab and Muslim Worlds, but the entire free world as well.

During the ascendant years of radical Arab socialism, Saudi Arabia sought to moderate its secular appeal by encouraging broader Islamic unity. The Islamic World League and the Organization of the Islamic Conference, both of which it sponsored, are examples of the policy.

In practical terms, the greatest contact between the Kingdom and the rest of the Arab World, then and now, was the annual pilgrimage, to which pilgrims from all over the Arab World attend annually. During the 1960s and 1970s, when radical Arab socialism was popular, Saudi Arabia refused to allow the Hajj to be used as a platform for secular intra-Arab politics. It did allow attacks against communism, however, which it saw as the greatest threat to the Muslim World and the hearts and minds of Muslims everywhere.

With the eclipse of radical Arab nationalism, Saudi Arabia has become a leading voice for moderation in the Arab World. Beginning with the Fahd Plan, it has also taken a more active role in seeking a solution to the Arab-Israeli conflict, one that would provide adequate security for Israel and justice for the Arab Palestinians who have been denied the right of self-determination for over a half-century.

Iran has dealt with the Arab World in a very different way. The Pahlavi Shahs saw both pan-Islamism and pan-Arabism as threats. Reza Shah tried to downplay Islam entirely, seeking to create a modern, secular state on Western lines, and during the Nasser period, Mohammad Reza Shah also saw secular Arab nationalism as a major threat to their ambitions to become the leading political power through the entire Middle East. Nevertheless, Reza Shah had fairly good relations with the Egyptian monarchy, marrying his son to the daughter of King Fouad (and sister of King Farouq, the last Egyptian King). Following the overthrow of the Egyptian monarchy by Jamal Abd Al-Nasser in 1952, Mohammad Reza Shah sought to exploit US antipathy toward Egyptian President Nasser and his doctrine of Arab socialism, justifying his never-ending arms requests to Washington on grounds that Iran was the first line of defense against the Soviet threat to the Middle East via its surrogates, the radical Arabs.

Despite mutual antipathy for communism with the conservative states of the Arabian Peninsula, Mohammad Reza Shah had tense relations with the Arab Gulf countries. National aspirations to be a predominant regional power were at that time centered close to home, and he claimed sovereignty over large offshore areas of the Arab side of the Gulf as well as the entire country of Bahrain. Relations improved in 1971 when he conceded to the Bahraini wishes for being an independent state. But when to compensate for not gaining sovereignty over Bahrain he unilaterally seized three islands belonging to UAE emirates - the Greater and Lesser Tunbs, which belong to Ras Al-Khaymah, and Abu Musa, which belongs to Sharjah - the stage was set for continued tensions over the sovereignty of the Islands.

Republican Iran has shown little inclination to improve relations with the Arab World as a whole, but as a revolutionary state seeking to export radical Islamist doctrines rather than as a conservative, pro-Western state opposing radical Arab nationalism, as was the case under the Shahs. It has three major policy goals in the Arab World that are not mutually exclusive. They are: exporting their Islamist revolution to replace moderate and Arab nationalist regimes with militant Islamic ones; political hegemony over the Gulf; and, in the case of Saudi Arabia, to neutralize any influence it might have in the Muslim World which it sees as a threat to its ambition to be the dominant Islamic power in the world. In all three cases, it is difficult to see where Iran's devotion to its radical Islamist doctrines leave off and its age-old national ambitions for regional hegemony begin, particularly closest to home in the Arab Gulf.

Following the Iranian revolution in Iran in 1979, Iran started attacking the Arab Gulf States and accusing them of being lackeys of Western imperialism. Khomeini, the spiritual leader of Iran, met with his close supporters and divided the Arab Gulf States among them. He perceived the Arab Gulf States as 'cantons and puppets' of the Western powers. He believed that he would be able to dominate them in a few years, and instructed Iranian ambassadors and intelligence personnel in the Arab Gulf countries to collect information on these States with the idea of creating Iranian hegemony throughout the Gulf.

Iran's two main targets in the Gulf were Saudi Arabia, which Khomeini believed was the biggest threat to Iranian hegemony over the Gulf and the entire Muslim World, and Bahrain, which has a Shi'ite majority and which Iran had claimed as its territory until the Shah conceded to the wishes of the Bahraini people for independence in 1971. Iran has also sought to undermine the regimes in Kuwait and the United Arab Emirates as well.

Saudi Arabia has always been viewed in Tehran as Iran's major rival in its efforts to become the leader of the Muslim World. Iran has supported subversive activities against the regime, principally among the Shi'ite minority, but also by Sunni dissidents as well. It has provided financial support and political indoctrination to Shi'ite groups in the Kingdom's Eastern Province, and has granted clandestine scholarships to Shi'ite students to study in Tehran, Isfahan, and Qum. These students would go first to Syria where they would check with the Iranian embassy to receive travel and identity documents, and then go on to Iran, leaving their Saudi passports behind.

Iran has not only supported subversive activities against the regime, but has tried to discredit the Kingdom with the entire Muslim World by orchestrating riots during the Hajj. It refuses to recognize Saudi Arabia as the 'Custodian of the two Holy Shrines, Makkah and Al-Madinah,' asserting that Saudi Arabia occupied them by force in 1924-1926. It claims that the Holy Places belong to the entire Muslim World and must be internationalized. Implicit in this position is the desire both to strip Saudi Arabia of its sacred trust, and then seek to dominate them itself.

In Bahrain, Khomeini considered restating the Iranian claim to sovereignty, but Iran ultimately decided to concentrate on replacing the Sunni regime under the Al Khalifah family with a Shi'ite regime.[6]

Regarding the United Arab Emirates and its quarrel with Iran on the three islands, when the 1971 agreement by Iran postponing the sovereignty issue expired in 1991[7], the Emirates asked Iran to return the islands to its custody, but Iran refused, citing its historic claim to the Islands. The two countries meet from time to time to discuss the problem but no solution appears to be in sight. For one thing, the issue remains a club with which Iran can seek to intimidate the Emirates politically when it appears to be in its interest to do so.

Kuwait was another early target of Iranian interference in its internal affairs. From the beginning, it supported anti-regime opposition parties, financed terrorist groups inside Kuwait, and concentrated on creating a fifth column among the Shi'ite minority. Many Kuwaiti Shi'ites have gone to Tehran and Qum for indoctrination in Iran's revolutionary Islamic ideology. The Iranian aim behind these activities was to export its revolution to Kuwait, which it still has not abandoned. To thwart Iranian efforts, Saudi Arabia increased security cooperation with Kuwaiti security services against Iranian-supported subversive activities inside the country.

The Iraq-Iran war, which started in 1980, temporarily halted Iran's subversive activities in the Arabian Peninsula. Nevertheless, Saudi Arabia continued to watch Iran's misbehavior with an open eye, and supported Iraq during the Iran-Iraq war.[8] The Arab Gulf countries followed suit, especially Kuwait. Most of them severed diplomatic relations with Iran, including Saudi Arabia. Throughout the war (1980-1988), relations between Iran and the Arab Gulf countries were strained and tense, with the exception of the Sultanate of Oman, which continued to have fairly good relations with Iran. As soon as the war ended, Saudi Arabia and the other Arab Gulf countries normalized relations with Iran and resumed diplomatic relations with it. Relations were still not cordial, but were much less tense than before as the primary threat to the Gulf States shifted to Iraq. The Iraqi invasion of Kuwait in 1990 was the straw that broke the camel's back.

Iran's subversive activities in the rest of the Arab World concentrated more on overthrowing existing regimes than on direct political hegemony, and have continued despite occasional overtures to the Arab States for better relations as Iran's economic conditions have deteriorated. The new Iranian regime quickly started helping the dissident opposition throughout the Arab World, seeking to topple moderate and conservative regimes alike in the name of Islamic revolution.   In Lebanon, it established a revolutionary Shi'ite organization, Hizballah (the Party of Allah). Its hundreds of thousands members have been indoctrinated to die if necessary in protecting Iran's interests in Lebanon and elsewhere. The Iranian support to Hizballah continues until today and it includes logistic, training and financial support.

In Egypt, Iran supported the terrorist groups with logistic and financial aid, as well as providing them paramilitary training in the Sudan. Egyptians and others were also brought for indoctrination in radical Islamist ideology to Qum, considered by the regime to be a holy Islamic city and the site of many religious activities. These activities were aimed at turning Egypt into a radical Islamist State.

In the Sudan, Iran, with the cooperation of the radical Islamist regime that came to power in Khartoum in 1987, helped turn the country into a training ground for Islamist terrorists from all over the Arab and Muslim Worlds, teaching them how to use weapons and explosives to carry out terrorist attacks. The Sudanese government, which was essentially a mix of a radical Islamist revolutionaries and a traditional military dictatorship, claimed to oppose terrorism, but had in fact chosen it as a tool for creating radical Islamist states throughout the region, with the idea that Sudan would be a major actor in Islamic World politics.

Iran has also been active in North Africa where radical Islamist groups have been active for many years. Because of Iran's direct financial and logistical support to Algerian terrorist groups, the Algerian government condemned Iran and severed diplomatic relations with it.   The Iranians have also extended support to subversive Islamist groups in Tunisia, training them in terrorist techniques in the Sudan.   After discovering these activities, the Tunisian government has warned Iran to cease its support.

The Iranian government also created clandestine training camps for Islamist terrorists groups in the Yemen Arab Republic. In the beginning, the Yemeni authorities believed that the trainees were innocent people who had been exiled by their own countries for political reasons. But finally, they discovered that they are terrorists who came to Yemen to receive training. The Yemeni government then launched a deportation campaign against those groups and deported them from the country.

Iran was also active in exporting their Islamist revolution to Syria, a close ally of Iran. Syria is a predominantly Sunni country whose ruling elite is Alawite, an offshoot of Shi'ism, and with the acquiescence of the Syrian government, Iranian teachers have moved openly inside Syria to spread Shi'ism. They have induced many Syrian villages, have changed their faith,[9] and have even induced some of the leading officers into Shi'ism. They have also introduced an old Twelver institution, the Mut'ah, a temporary marriage contract for the purpose of pleasure, which has become very popular in Syria. Many Iranian clerics have defended the Mut'ah as morally preferable to the open promiscuity practiced in the West. Shi'ite influence has increased tremendously inside the Shi'ite neighborhoods near the al-Sayyidah Zainab Mosque in Damascus, and the construction of Shi'ite religious schools throughout the country has increased also. The government will not, however, allow Iranian activities that it sees as a threat to its own security. When Iran asked permission to form a Syrian Hizballah, the Syrian government refused the request. All in all, however, the relations between Syria and Iran are excellent and the two countries are close allies.

The contrast between the Iranian approach to the Arab World and the Saudi approach is quite clear. In essence, Iran's first priority is to exporting the Iranian revolution. This preoccupation stems from the depth of Shi'ite thinking and is considered by the regime to be imperative for its survival. It is aimed at both securing the revolutionary gains abroad and maintaining the stability of the regime at home. In a clearly summed up statement by Homayoun Moqaddam, an official in Bazargan's government, he said the Iranian regime's strategy after the second Gulf war is training terrorists and those elements who are willing to conduct terrorist and military operations in the Gulf and the Yemen Arab Republic.[10] Furthermore, Iranian Radio and Television Service has established forty-five radio and television stations to broadcast the voice of the Islamic Republic of Iran to reach the five continents.[11] Iran has allocated US$396 million to support Shi'ite as well as Sunni opposition groups and parties outside Iran to strengthen them and help them topple their own governments.[12] And to further ideological indoctrination, Shi'ite students from around the world are offered scholarships to study in Tehran, Shiraz and Qum.

Saudi Arabia's approach to the Arab World, on the other hand, attempts to create harmony, peace, and concord, not subversion and conflict. It strives to promote both Arab unity as well as Islamic unity. In contrast, to Iran's efforts to create conflict, Saudi Arabia has tried on a number of occasions to mediate between Arab governments and opposition groups, notably in Algeria. Unfortunately it could not produce any positive results. The Saudi government has also never attempted to export its political system under the guise of building Islamic schools or mosques or tried to build a school or a mosque without the full agreement and cooperation of the host government. Its financial support abroad is focused on economic projects and Islamic endowments, not on interfering in the internal affairs of brother Arab and Muslim States.

From the Saudi point of view, cooperation is always preferable to confrontation and it has always been willing to seek a peaceful resolution to outstanding problems with Iran concerning its policies and those of neighboring States. Occasionally it has succeeded, but where it has not, it has been forced to stand up against Iran and counter its policies and activities in the Arab and Muslim World. The competition has been fierce and the challenge was very difficult, but the Kingdom is convinced that it is the right way.

Saudi Arabia, Iran and South Asia:

Aside from Iran, South Asia includes the countries of India, Pakistan, Bangladesh, Sri Lanka and Afghanistan. India, although it is the largest country in the region with a large Muslim minority, is dominated politically by its Hindu majority and is therefore not politically a part of the Muslim World. Aside from mutual concern over the welfare of Indian Muslims, and the potential threat of its possession of weapons of mass destruction, there is little Saudi-Iranian confrontation or cooperation regarding India. Nevertheless, South Asia is an important region for both Saudi Arabia and Iran, and both have tried to influence events there, although in very different ways.

Pakistan is considered a pivotal State. It was the first Islamic country to stand against the Iranian exportation of its revolution.[13] Pakistan is predominantly Sunni, with a 12 to 15 percent Shi'ite minority.

Pakistan, the first modern republic with an Islamic constitution, is a pivotal State in the Islamic foreign policies of both Saudi Arabia and Iran. Saudi-Pakistani relations go back over fifty years to Pakistan's independence from British colonialism. Saudi

Arabia has contributed to the development plan of Pakistan and has assisted Pakistan financially and morally. Politically, Saudi Arabia has helped Pakistan in its dispute with India on the Kashmiri issue and on their border problem. Militarily, Saudi Arabia has stood beside Pakistan in its 1965 and 1971 wars with India, and cooperated closely with Pakistan in opposing the Marxist government in Kabul during the Afghan war. Economically, Saudi Arabia has opened its border to Pakistanis who come to work on Saudi soil, resulting in billions of dollars of transfer payments back to Pakistan. Saudi Arabia has also sent religious teachers to Pakistan, with the agreement of the Pakistani government, and has built hundreds of mosques and religious schools and associations throughout the country, and has sent millions of copies of the Quran and religious books to the country. Therefore, the religious relations between the two countries were well established since the creation of Pakistan.

Saudi relations with Pakistan have always been based on mutual agreement with the Pakistani government. The Kingdom has never forced its aid or its teachings on another society. This is inherent in King Fahd's stated message to the Islamic World: "We will not interfere in anyone's affairs against their wishes and will not tolerate interference in our affairs without our agreement." The King wanted to stress and reconfirm this point as a basic tenet of Saudi Islamic foreign policy.

Iran, on the other hand, had no tradition of religious relations with Pakistan. During the reign of Mohammad Reza Shah, Iranian-Pakistani relations were focused on economic and military affairs. For example, they created a joint Regional Cooperation Organization (RCO) and also joined several regional organizations for cooperation in the area of mutual security. But there were no religious ties between the two countries. This was in large part because Iran is predominantly Shi'ite, whereas Pakistan is predominantly Sunni with a Shi'ite minority of about 12 to 15 percent of the population. Moreover, the Shah wanted to create a secular state and sought to de-emphasize religion entirely.

The situation changed rapidly after the 1979 revolution in Iran. The new regime set out at once to create a Shi'ite theocracy at home and to export their revolution abroad. Very quickly, it established close ties with the Shi'ite minority in Pakistan, providing it with financial assistance and building Shi'ite mosques, schools and Husayniyas (Shi'ite religious, social and community centers) and hospitals. It also granted Shi'ite students scholarships to study Shi'ism in Tehran, Qum and other Iranian cities.

Iran became directly involved in Pakistani politics, contributing financially to a political campaign to put more Shi'ite leaders in the forefront of Pakistani parliament and the Pakistani political life. It also financed the violent groups inside Pakistan and incited Shi'ite militants to rise up against their own government. With Iranian encouragement, Shi'ite militants demanded more Shi'ite participation in the political system, despite the fact that there were no differences between Sunnis and Shi'ites in the Pakistani society. Prior to 1979, there was very little sectarian discord in the country and most Shi'ites were not heavily involved in politics.

Iran's objective was nothing less that to turn Pakistan into a radical Shi'ite state, converting the Sunnis to Twelver Islam. To meet this objective, it established an organization called 'The Association for Implementing Ja'fari Fiqh (Twelver Islamic Jurisprudence)' in Pakistan and appointed Mohammad Taqi Naqavi as the Vice President in charge of conducting the Shi'ite affairs in Pakistan, including running the schools and other facilities of the association. To meet this objective, it continues to build Shi'ite schools, Husayniyas, and mosques all over Pakistan. Its financial donations and its contributions to the new buildings for Shi'ites in Pakistan never stops. It also continues to provide paramilitary training for Shi'ite militants for a time when they can take over the country by force.

With such a large Sunni majority, the machinations of Iran failed. Moreover, the Pakistani government has moved quickly to stop Iran from interfering in its internal politics, and to prevent internal sectarian strife that Iran tried to stir up.

In Bangladesh and Sri-Lanka, the same differences in Saudi-Iranian approaches can be noted. Whereas Saudi Arabia acted peacefully, Iran actively interfered in their internal affairs. Saudi Arabia has provided economic assistance, including grants and non-interest bearing loans, and has built mosques, hospitals and religious schools and institutions, but all with the cooperation of the local governments and never as a means for interfering with the internal affairs of the countries. Iran has also provided economic assistance, but as a means of interfering in their domestic affairs. Due to the poor economic situation in both countries, they did not protest Iranian interference for fear of losing Iranian financial assistance and investment, which they greatly needed.

In Afghanistan, the story is much more complicated. The Saudi involvement in Afghanistan goes back to the communist take-over in 1979. In that year, Saudi Arabia, together with many other Muslim countries, as well as the United States, decided to support Afghan Muslim holy warriors (Mujahideen) in their efforts to topple the Marxist government and to expel Soviet troops from the country that kept it in power. The Saudis contributed US$500 million annually to that effort. Many Saudi citizens went to Pakistan to participate in the war against the Soviets, and many religious organizations also participated in that holy war. Among them were the Saudi Red Crescent Society, the Islamic World League and the Islamic Ighatha Organization.

Despite the overthrow of the Marxist regime in 1989, the internal situation has remained stormy in Afghanistan. Saudi Arabia has maintained its policy of seeking to help the war torn country and has sought to exert a moderating influence on the government while scrupulously avoiding any interference in Afghani internal affairs.

Iran's relations with neighboring Afghanistan go back hundreds of years. In fact, Dari, the leading language of Afghanistan, is an offshoot of Persian. In the 1920s, the two countries almost went to war over Hirat, an Afghani province that borders Iran. Iranian-Afghani relations were tense during the reign of Reza Shah Pahlavi, and continued to be so during the reign of his son, Mohammad Reza Shah. Iran did not contribute to the liberation of Afghanistan from communism during the years of Afghan War, but it did receive many of the Afghani refugees.

When the republican regime came to power in Iran, relations deteriorated even more. Tehran inaugurated a policy of providing financial and military assistance to Afghanistan's Shi'ite community who make up about ten percent of the total population and virtually all of whom are members of the Hazara tribe. In time, Iran also began providing arms, ammunition, financial assistance, and logistics to other groups opposed to the new, legitimate government of Afghanistan. For example, it has sent officers from the Iranian Revolutionary Guards to Tikhar province to train the opposition in insurgency tactics. In fact, Iran has been instrumental in prolonging the Afghani civil war that is pulling the country apart. The warring parties depend on outside logistical and financial support and Iran is a critical source.

Saudi Arabia, on the other hand, has been trying to stop the civil war. In 1995, it was able to gather all the warring parties together in Makkah, where a cease fire agreement was reached. One month later, however, the fighting resumed.

Saudi Arabia, Iran and South-East Asia:

Prior to the Islamic revolution in 1979, Iran took little or no interest in South-East Asia. Saudi Arabia was the major contributor to the Islamic projects in the region, including the building of mosques, Islamic schools and hospitals, and the establishment of Islamic religious, social and educational organizations.

After 1979, the story changed. Consonant with its policy of spreading its Islamic revolution, Iran moved rapidly to establish ties with Muslim communities in South East Asian countries such as Malaysia, Indonesia, Thailand, and Singapore. At first it extended support to Shi'ite minorities. But these communities were too small to force the political changes it had in mind, so she expanded its operations to Sunnis as well, seeking to indoctrinate them with the Shi'ite revolution. For example, it offered scholarships to Sunni students to study in Tehran, Isfahan, and Qum. After graduating, they would be sent back home to spread the Shi'ite doctrines. It also tried to incite the Muslim community in southern Thailand to rise up against the government in Bangkok, training hundreds of them in the use of explosives and light weapons for use in a full-fledged insurgency.

All these efforts by Iran were carefully monitored by Saudi Arabia. But the Saudis were so patient; they did not try to stop Iranian plots with plots of their own. Instead, they offered help and assistance to the local citizens. As they have done in other parts of the Muslim World, they tried to help the people directly. Financially, they sent both official aid and guaranteed interest-free loans, and also encouraged private financial donations (Zakat) from their citizens; religiously, they built mosques and sent religious scholars and religious books, including the Holy Quran; culturally, they built Islamic centers and established Islamic organizations; and educationally, they built Islamic schools.

In the end, helping people to better themselves is a far greater contribution than seeking to tear down government institutions and creating social confrontations. Thus, without trying to acquire political influence, Saudi policy has been far more helpful in South East Asia than Iranian policies.

Saudi Arabia, Iran and Africa *(See Chapter Five)*:

Historically, Africa, with the exception of the Arab states, already discussed above, was never a major factor in Saudi-Iranian relations with the Muslim World. The reason for this is that Iran never showed much interest in Muslim Africa south of the Sahara. We have mentioned Iran's interest in the Sudan, which is sub-Saharan geographically, but it is seen by Iran as basically Arab. The only other sub-Saharan country to elicit much Iranian interest is Nigeria, but that interest is limited to oil matters, as Nigeria is a major OPEC country.

By contrast, the territories that now constitute Saudi Arabia have had ongoing relations with sub-Saharan Africa for centuries. For centuries, they purchased slaves and other commodities from East Africa to ports on the Red Sea and the Arabian Gulf (including Persian ports). Slavery has been outlawed in modern times, but it was never the barbaric institution that it was in the West.

Arabia's greatest contact with Africans, however, was religious: through the Hajj. For hundreds of years, African pilgrims coming to Makkah have literally walked across the continent to the Red Sea coast, and then obtained passage by ship to Jeddah, the gateway to Makkah. Even in modern times, this migration has been a key economic factor for the countries they transited, for the Hajjis would find work along the way to finance their trek, sometimes taking years to get there. For many years, West African Hajjis picked most of the cotton crop in the Sudan, a major foreign exchange earner, on the way to Makkah. Once in the Hijaz, African Hajjis would again stay on for long periods to earn enough money for the return trip. This practice has now ended with the advent of modern transportation, but it has left behind a legacy of religious relations that have lasted to this day.

Africa has continued to be a major focus of Saudi religious

policy in recent years. An early prompter of that policy was King Faysal, who visited the continent twice, once in 1966 and again in 1972. On his first trip, he visited Mali and Guinea.[14] On his second, he visited Uganda, Chad, Senegal, Mauritania, Guinea.[15] King Faysal promoted Islamic unity and also convinced many of the African countries to cut their ties with Israel as an enemy of Islam. Twenty-eight African states subsequently severed diplomatic relations with Israel.[16]

Bilateral relations with the Kingdom were also strengthened. Ministerial visits between the two countries were increased, trade relations were expanded, and the Saudis increased their financial assistance to those countries. In what became the pattern for future Saudi policy in the Muslim World, the Kingdom also constructed hospitals, schools and religious institutions.

A major factor of the success of Saudi relations with sub-Saharan Africa was that the Kingdom did not proceed from the intention of political or economic gain. It was simply seeking to enhance Islamic unity and to seek common cause with fellow Muslim communities to increase the economic and spiritual welfare of their citizens. Relations at the government-to-government level were always conducted with mutual respect and cordiality.

This is not to say that bilateral relations with all the Muslim States of sub-Saharan Africa were continually cordial. Bilateral relations, even between friendly states, are bound to have ups and downs. For example, Saudi assistance to the Sudan and Somalia has been generous. But when they, and particularly Somalia engaged in very cordial relations with the Soviet Union, considered by Saudi Arabia to be atheistic and anti-Islamic, bilateral relations became strained. The Kingdom worked hard at persuading Somalia to rally with the Muslim World in the struggle against communism. In time, it did so and bilateral relations improved.

Soon after the 1979 revolution, Iran began to take a new interest in the African continent. Seeking to export its revolution and spread Shi'ism, Iran sent economic and diplomatic missions all over the continent, offering financial aid and arranging cultural exchanges. These efforts were coordinated by a newly established 'African High Council,' based in the Iranian Presidential Office, and tasked with developing political, cultural and economic relationships with the

African States, and following up on all agreements signed with African States.(17)

Mali is a good example of how Iran has courted African states. In order to develop closer economic ties with Mali, Iran persuaded it to form a joint economic commission in February 1997. The stated aim of the committee is to boost trade relations between the two countries, including the export of Iranian industrial materials and goods to Mali. Although for Mali the commission probably represents an opportunity to encourage more economic aid, for Iran it is an opportunity to expand its political influence.

As evidence of Iran's new interest in Africa, it has doubled the number of its diplomatic missions in the continent which now number 25 and are accredited to almost 40 countries.(18) Politically, it portrays itself as a peacemaker in Africa, attempting to mediate disputes between the Sudan and Uganda, and between Libya and Sierra Leon.(19)

In fact, however, Iran's aims are much broader. They include four secular goals and three Islamist goals. The secular goals are: 1) to promote itself as a leader in the developing world; 2) to gain support in the international foray such as the United Nations, particularly over issues concerning its international political isolation and perceived encirclement by the Western powers; 3) to pursue legitimate economic interests; and 4) to promote itself as an alternative to Western powers for development assistance. The Islamist goals are: 1) to export its brand of Islamic revolution; 2) to spread Shi'ite doctrine and its interpretation of Islamic law; and 3) Iran's overarching political as well as Islamist goal which permeates all Iranian foreign policy, to propel itself to the position of the most powerful Muslim state and leader of the Muslim World.

To accomplish its aims, Iran employs much the same strategy as it uses in other poor regions. Africa is an impoverished continent; illiteracy, malnutrition and disease are endemic. The African states desperately need economic assistance from anywhere they can get it. Iran cynically offers assistance, but with conditions. It wants a free hand to spread its political influence and its Shi'ite revolution through proselytization and the building of Shi'ite mosques, schools and cultural centers.

Iran's policies in Africa have had very mixed results. In Mali and the Ivory Coast, for example, it has been moderately successful. In Nigeria, on the other hand, although it has a huge Muslim population, Iranian policies have failed completely. All in all, Saudi Arabia, by limiting its aims to assisting the cultural and spiritual needs of African Muslims without pushing a political agenda has yielded far more results. *(See Chapter Five)*

Saudi Arabia, Iran and Central Asia:

Central Asia is the latest region in which Iran sees itself in competition with Saudi Arabia for influence. Until the collapse of the Soviet Union in 1989 opened Central Asia to the outside world it was one of the least known regions on earth. The Soviets completely dominated the region's political systems, economies, societies and culture. Except for a few visits by tourists under the auspices of the Soviet government, an occasional Western technocrat, the region was generally off limits to most foreigners.

Central Asia has a long and glorious history as a center of Islamic culture and learning, however, the years of Sovietization failed to totally erase centuries of the region's ties with the rest of the Muslim World. When the former Islamic Soviet Republics regained their independence from Moscow, it was only natural that they would look again toward the south as well as to the West. Responding to these overtures was not only Saudi Arabia and Iran, but also Turkey.

Turkey has historic ties with Central Asia. Portions of the region had at one time been a part of the Ottoman Empire, and Sunnis throughout the region had recognized the Ottoman Caliph as their spiritual leader. Turkey is a secular state, however, and its contemporary interests in Central Asia are predominantly secular, not religious. It has strong security interests with countries near or on its borders, and has economic interests in opening up trade relations and possible oil pipelines from the former Soviet republics. In addition, the original Turks migrated from the Turkmen areas of Central Asia and share ethnic, linguistic and cultural ties with them.[20]

Iran also borders on Central Asia and has strong secular, political, security and economic interests as well. Thus, they viewed Turkey as a major rival for gaining political and economic influence in Central Asia. But because Turkey is a secular state, Iranian competition with Turkey was primarily secular rather than religious, despite the fact that the age-old rivalry between Sunni Turkey and Shi'ite Iran did add a sectarian element to otherwise secular politics.

This was not the case regarding Saudi Arabia. The Kingdom is geographically far removed from Central Asia and has no political agenda with respect to the Muslim countries there. Its ties are mainly religious and even during the Soviet period, a few Muslims, almost entirely from Central Asia, were allowed to make the Hajj, and in some cases were allowed to make contact with relatives there, which Moscow hoped could be used to its benefit. There is a large community of Central Asian Muslims in Saudi Arabia, often called by the generic name, 'Tashkandis', who heroically fled Soviet persecution in the 1920s and ended up in the Kingdom. Needless to say, they are intensely anti-communist. Despite no grounds for competition, however, Iran considered Saudi Arabia a major threat to its efforts to extend its political, economic and religious influence in Central Asia.

Saudi Arabia, unlike Iran, had no diplomatic relations with the Soviet Union, and neither country, of course, were allowed to have official contacts with the former Soviet Republics of Central Asia. Following their independence, both countries established diplomatic relations, but Iran also moved very fast to create a strong power base in those countries. In addition to trying to expand political and economic ties, it worked hard to create a strong religious presence as well, quickly establishing ties with local religious groups without distinguishing between Sunnis and Shi'ites.

Despite the fact that its own domestic economy was in shambles, Iran lavished foreign aid on the newly independent Central Asian States. Among the projects managed and run by the Iranians were the rebuilding and renovation of the Islamic sites in Turkmenistan and Georgia; building a hospital and medical laboratory in Turkmenistan as well as desalination plants at Maro, Khaywah, and Ashkhabad, the capital; developing modern farms in Tajikistan; housing projects in Kirghizstan; building a desalination plant in Kazakhstan; the establishment of modern communication lines and an electric generating plant in Azerbaijan; and the renovation of mosques and religious schools in Azerbaijan.[21]

Over 2000 Iranians were sent to participate in these projects, including engineers, advisers, and skilled labors.[22] However, they also included about 50 Iranian intelligence officers assigned as project advisors, but who are really tasked with covertly exporting their revolution and collecting information on their target countries to send back to Tehran.[23]

In addition to religious and economic development projects, Iran has also sought to develop closer ties between local universities and the Iranian Ministries of Higher Education and Information, creating exchange programs and offering fellowships for study in Iran. In one such exchange program, for example, about 37 students and 14 teachers traveled to Iran to study Persian literature.

These activities confirm a pattern observed elsewhere. Iran seeks to become the principal influence in political, religious, economic and social affairs in these countries, with the broader aim of becoming the leading regional political power and the leading Islamic power throughout the entire Muslim World. To accomplish these aims, they seek to cement ties with local political, religious, and commercial leaders, and offer financial aid for development of social, economic and religious projects. They then exploit these projects to infiltrate the country for spreading their Islamist revolution and Shi'ite doctrines.

Iranian activities in Central Asia, however, also display an increased sophistication and pragmatism from the early days of the Iranian Republic. Instead of concentrating their covert and overt activities only on Shi'ite communities, they now seek to reach potential Sunnis as well, particularly where too much overt concentration on Shi'ite doctrines is counter-productive among Sunni majorities. Because only a small minority of Muslims are Shi'ites, the only way they could hope to become the leader of the Muslim World is to appeal to all Muslims, Sunni as well as Shi'ite.

Saudi relations with Central Asia also followed a pattern practiced elsewhere by offering help without interfering in the internal affairs of another State, and an emphasis on strengthening Islamic values without insisting on a particular ideology or Madhhab. The Central Asian countries needed all the help they could get. After years of Soviet domination the Central Asian countries were ill prepared to rule themselves or manage their economies, many of which are still closely tied to the Russian economy, and some still rely on Russian Federation currency. In the area of public administration, some states are still dependent on the Russian Federation in managing their day to day affairs. Saudi Arabia has tried to help with financial aid and economic and social development assistance, but it will still take many years for some of these countries to gain the experience to govern their own affairs with efficiency and justice.

Although the great majority of Central Asians are nominally Muslim, their knowledge of Islam and its practices is barely existent after decades of state enforced atheism. Many of the people no longer even knew how to pray, one of five basic pillars of fundamentals of Islam.[24] In addition, although many had copies of the Quran in their homes, few knew how to recite it, an important act of worship. Only a few could read or speak Arabic, the language of the Quran and important source books on Islam. Those few, who studied the language abroad in Egypt, Syria or Jordan, were called Muftis, authorities on Islamic law, no matter how much or little they had actually studied the Shari'a.

Saudi Arabia has made a concerted effort to bring the religion back to the people, building and restoring mosques, building Islamic schools and inviting Islamic students to study in the Kingdom. All this has been done with the blessing of the local governments, however. Its motive was not to position the governments closer to Saudi Arabia, but to bring the people back closer to Allah. That, in short is the essence of Saudi Arabia's Islamic foreign policy.

FOOTNOTES

(1)   Saeed M. Badeeb, 'Saudi-Iranian Relations (1932-1982)', (London: Center for Arab and Iranian Studies and Echoes,1993), p.7678.

(2)   The Sunna is the deeds and traditions of Prophet Mohammad (Peace Be Upon Him), and with the Quran constitutes the sources of the Holy Law, Shari'a.

(3)   'This is Our Country', Ministry of Information, Kingdom of Saudi Arabia, 1991.

(4)   Badeeb, 'Saudi-Iranian Relations (1932-1982)', p. 7475.

(5)   Ibid., pp.76-78.

(6)   The Voice of America, A speech by Dr. Jamal Al-Suwaidi, Director, Emirates Center for Strategic Studies and Research, October, 6, 1997.

(7)   Abu Musa belongs to the Emirate of Al-Sharjah, and the two Tunbs belong to the Emirate of Ras AlKhaymah.

(8)   The total Saudi support for Iraq in its war with Iran was about US$28 billion, plus some logistic support.

(9)   Although Shi'ites are a minority in Syria, the ruling elite are Alawite, and offshoot of Shi'ism.

(10) Interview with Ahmed Ra'ed, London, May 10, 1997.

(11) Ibid.

(12) Ibid.

(13) Interview with a senior Pakistani diplomat who did not want his name to be mentioned. Jeddah, Saudi Arabia, 9 February 1994.

(14) Mohammad Diab, 'Al-Faisal Fil-Ma'rakah', (Faisal is in The Battle), (Beirut, Dar al-Sha'b, 1975), pp.28-33.

(15) Ibid.

(16) Ibid., p.25.

(17) Interview with a Nigerian Army General, Lagos, May 1998.

(18) Ibid.

(19) Ibid.

(20) Turkey was one of the first countries to seek closer ties with the newly independent Muslim states of Central Asia. With its historic ethnic and religious ties and its non-threatening policies, its policies have met with a great deal of success.

(21) Information based on materials obtained during an interview with
     Ahmed Ra'ed, London, November 1996.

(22) Ibid.

(23) Ibid.

(24) Prayer is divided into two parts. The first part is FARDH, i.e.,
     obligatory prayer. This is performed compulsory five times a day.
     The second part is SUNNAH. This is prayed either after or before
     the FARDH prayer. It is only two Sajdah. The Muslim act of prayer
     involves well defined execution of certain required acts: the Ghusl,
     or spiritual and physical cleansing; the Niyah, a statement of
     intention; the Raqa', bending the back; and the Sajdah, prostration.
     The prayers themselves, said during or between the required
     sequence and number of these acts are divided into two parts. The
     first part is obligatory, Fardh, and is performed five times a day.
     The second is Holy Tradition, Sunna, the traditions of the Prophet,
     and can be said either before or after the obligatory prayer.

CHAPTER THREE

Saudi Arabia, Iran and the Western World

The relationship between Saudi Arabia, the Islamic Republic of Iran and the Western World is a complicated relationship. This relationship has had its ups and downs, particularly with regard to Iran after its 1979 revolution against the Shah. In fact, Iran has followed a very harsh, violent and strict policy vis a vis the Western World. It also tried to export its revolution to the Islamic and Western World. This situation has lasted for almost seventeen years, i.e. from 1979 to 1996. In 1997, however, Iran changed from the inside. A wise statesman, Mohammad Khatami was elected to the presidency. He was elected by the younger generation of Iran. That generation wanted to have a real change in the political, social, and economic life of the country. That generation wanted to have a president who would solve their social and economic problems. They also wanted to have a president who understood the structure of the World's political and economic policies. The new President would, therefore, choose a modern and experienced cabinet. That cabinet would, ultimately, run the country in a democratic and liberal way.

Europe, nevertheless, was divided into East and West. The Eastern European countries are nineteen states. The Western European countries are fifteen States. Before 1990, most of the Eastern European countries were either under the full control of the Soviet Union, or under its influence. The Western European countries were under a free and democratic system. Prior to the 1979 Iranian revolution, Iran had a diplomatic relationship with few Eastern European countries. Saudi Arabia, however, had no diplomatic relationship with any Eastern European country. After the collapse of the Soviet Union in 1990, Saudi Arabia had recognized many of the Eastern European countries and had established diplomatic relationship with them, including the Russian Federation.

51

Both Iran and Saudi Arabia have had good relationships with the Western European countries. Historically, Saudi Arabia had cut, briefly, its diplomatic relationship with France and Great Britain after the 1956 tripartite attack on Egypt, or the so-called Suez Canal War. However, Iran had a different relationship with the Western European countries, which will be discussed later in this chapter, particularly after the 1979 revolution.

After the election of Khatami as President, Iran began to develop a new policy of rapprochement with the Western World. As a matter of fact, Khatami sought to turn from an enemy to a friend. He expressed a willingness to have a peaceful relationship with the Western World. That relationship was to be based on mutual respect and mutual interest. Nevertheless, these efforts were slowed down by the most radical and extreme elements of the Mullahs or the ruling elites of Iran. In fact, Iran wanted to establish that relationship due to a number of reasons:

(1) to break the political isolation that it puts herself in.

(2) to bridge the bad economic situation of the country.

(3) to reestablish the ordinary social life with the West.

(4) to reschedule its financial debts to the West.

(5) to prove to the West that she is a peace loving country.

In the meantime, and since the election of President Mohammad Khatami, Iran has decided to reduce tension between itself and the outside World. She also has decided to broaden its friendly relationships with other countries in the region and the outside World. This policy, according to the Interior minister of Iran, has emanated from the strong beliefs that:

(a) Iran does not have any ambitions.
(b) Iran does not have any foreign greediness.
(c) Iran is sincerely planning to integrate itself into a balanced and just system in the region and the world as a whole.

As a matter of fact, and after the period of Ayatollah Khomeini, Iran has been very much concerned with its outside image, particularly with the Western World, the Gulf region, and the Arab World. This has been very obvious with the coming of President Khatami to power in 1997. He was determined to change the image of Iran outside its borders. He was also willing to change Iran's relations with the Arabian/Persian Gulf region and with the Arab World. However, there were those who opposed him and his policies. Nevertheless, in Iran today there are two groups who make the policies of the country:

1) The Hardliners, and 2) the Moderates, or the so called 'Reformists'. The first group is under the influence of the revolution's supreme guide and he is Ayatollah Khamenei. The hardliners generally control the constitution, the Army, the Revolutionary Guards, the General Intelligence, and the General Security forces. They also control the Judiciary and the Parliamentary wings of Iran's government. The second group is presided over by the President of the country who was elected by the people. He has executive authority and controls the Information apparatus. From the outset, both groups have struggled to gain influence and power in the country.[1]

As far as Saudi Arabia is concerned, she has had a very peaceful as well as a very fruitful relationship with the Western World. That relationship was and still is based on mutual respect and mutual interests. Historically speaking, the Kingdom of Saudi Arabia has had very successful diplomatic relations with the Western European countries. Even before its becoming a full autonomous Kingdom, she has had a very close relationship with the British Kingdom. The British had a 'Protection Agreement' with the Arab Gulf countries in 1899, with the exception of Saudi Arabia. Consequently, this has made King Abd Al-Aziz sign a number of treaties with the British Empire and have a good relationship with them.[2] The Iranian government was against the British presence in the Gulf region. They wanted to have full control and full hegemonies of the Arab Gulf countries. They even considered Bahrain as part of Iran.[3]

However, the Kingdom of Saudi Arabia has built its relations with the Western World since its creation in the year 1932. King Abd Al-Aziz was a peace-loving ruler. He did not want to have any dispute with the British or with any other Western power. After 1932, His majesty began to send his diplomats to the Western Capitals starting with Great Britain and the Republic of France. In fact, the Saudi Foreign Ministry was established in 1929, that is two years before the establishment of the Kingdom of Saudi Arabia. Nevertheless, we will focus on the major European countries and their bilateral relations with both Saudi Arabia and the Islamic Republic of Iran. These major countries are: 1) Great Britain, 2) The Republic of France, and 3) The German Republic. As a matter of fact, it is very difficult to cover all European countries, particularly that Europe is divided into East and West, despite the fact that we are covering Western Europe only. It is worth mentioning here that Iran accused the Western countries of following a 'dual standard' in the issues of human rights, terrorism, and arms control. Moreover, Iran wants to be a free country and wants to depend on herself alone. This is, in fact, the primary goal of the Iranian foreign policy.

Relations with Great Britain:

The relationship between Saudi Arabia, the Islamic Republic of Iran and Great Britain was to be characterized as 'a pull and push' relationship. After the Iranian 1979 revolution, the British government was not surprised, but shocked with the change in Iran. The Shah of Iran was a close friend of the British, and he had many treaties with them. It is even said that the Shah had occupied the three islands in the United Arab Emirates in 1971, after receiving the 'green light' from the British government.[4] However, the new Iranian government under the rule of Ayatollah Khomeini condemned the British government for its interference in the Gulf region's affairs. This sent the relationship between the two countries into a stalemate.

After the militant student uprising on 4 November 1979, and the capture of the American embassy's employees as hostages, the British government denounced this action as a violation of international law. Therefore, Britain decided to lower the diplomatic representation of Iran in Britain to a chargè d'affaires level. Consequently, the Iranian government did the same thing and lowered the British diplomatic level in Iran.[5] Throughout the war between Iraq and Iran (1980-1988), the British supported Iraq militarily, secretly and openly. Consequently, this action created a mutual mistrust and mutual doubts between the two countries. Nevertheless, the straw that broke the camel's back was the issue of Salman Rushdi, the Indian born British citizen who wrote a book denouncing the Holy Prophet Mohammad and badly characterizing and criticizing Ayatollah Khomeini. The Iranian government issued a 'Fatwa' on 15 February 1989, denouncing Salman Rushdi and issued a death sentence against him. In fact, the Iranian government was more angry from the criticisim of Ayatollah Khomeini than from the denunciation of the Prophet Mohammad, but they had combined the two issues into a religious pretext.

Moreover, Britain has accepted many Iranian refugees. Among those refugees were some ministers, a number of diplomats, a number of journalists, and a number of businessmen. This has caused anger among the new ruling elites in Iran. The political Iranian refugees in Britain are given a social guarantee and receive between 500-800 British Pounds on a monthly basis. The British government pays 1200 Pounds for every child of the political refugees for his or her education.[6] Moreover, there are two weekly newspapers that are produced in Britain for the Iranian opposition. These newspapers are Kayhan and Nimruz.[7] Also, there is a broadcasting system in London under the name 'Spectrum'. This system broadcasts a two-hour program, weekly, in Persian language. It attracts a lot of Iranian listeners.[8] In addition, there are three flights working on a weekly basis from Tehran to London. In fact, the rich Iranian citizens live in England and France. These Iranians have business relationship with their counterparts and businessmen in England as well as inside Iran. There are also plenty of Iranian shops in London and elsewhere in England. These shops are specialized in selling of rugs, furniture and other commodities.

In the mean time, the Iranian Intelligence Organization (MOIS) is very active inside Britain. It has a 'killing squad' inside London and in other European cities. As a matter of fact, this 'killing squad' was able to murder 35 personalities from the Iranian opposition in Europe. In the mean time, MOIS has its own agents in London and other European cities. These agents write their own intelligence reports and send it to Tehran on a daily and a weekly basis. They also write on the Iranian opposition activities and their moves. They also analyze their newspapers and magazines and write back to Tehran.

Militarily speaking, there are many British military experts working for the Iranian military industrial sectors such as tanks, helicopter, and conventional arms.[9] These British experts are not sent by the British government, but they are free-lancers who were brought in by the Iranian government and are well paid. However, the diplomatic relationship between the two countries was restored in 1998, and the two countries have resumed their full ties. The current relationship between the two countries includes political, economic, social, and diplomatic ties.

Regarding Saudi Arabia's relations with Great Britain since 1979, that relationship was excellent and very productive. The political, military, and economic cooperation between the two countries was and still is a very prominent relationship. The only setback in that relationship was caused by the British action of receiving Saudi religious extremists, opposition leaders, and the politically oriented anti Saudi citizens. For example, People like Mohammad El-Mas'ari, and Osama Faqih, were received by the British and were given the right to stay in London despite the Saudi demand to hand them over or to kick them out of Britain.[10] Many Saudi-British contacts were to take place, but without any positive results. In the Saudi eyes, this is a 'security problem' between the two countries. Welcoming and hosting the Saudi opposition in London and different British cities of Great Britain is something not acceptable to the Saudi government. In addition to that, there are a great number of newspapers, magazines, and videotapes against the Saudi monarchy, which are sold in Britain. The only British answer to the Saudi opposition is that: 'We don't have an information ministry'.

Economically speaking, the Saudi-British relationship is good. Saudi Arabia imports a number of electronics, ovens, refrigerators, and cars from Britain. There is also a society for Saudi-British friendship where a number of trade projects are discussed. Meanwhile, the United Kingdom is the second largest investor in the Saudi economy after the United States of America. There are also a number of joint-ventures between the two countries. Among those joint ventures is the Saudi-British Al-Yamamah project. This joint venture is basically a military one, but it has an economic side. The value of the project is a billion US dollars, and the project has a number of economic oriented programs. In October 1989, Prince Fahd Al-Abdullah, assistant to the Minister of Defense said:[11] "The investments under the programs were expected to exceed SR20 billion, (US$5.3 bn), and would provide 80,000 job opportunities. He added that: the most important consideration behind the 'Offset Program' is the investment scheme which was to enable Saudi firms to become internationally active and competitive."

In fact, these economic programs are affiliated with the 'Yamamah' joint venture and would serve the Saudi economy. The offset program itself is a product of the interests and the benefits of the project as a whole. Therefore, the 'Yamamah' joint-venture has a direct economic link and would contribute to the economy of Saudi Arabia.

Militarily, Saudi Arabia imports a number of defense equipment and spare parts from Great Britain. Among those equipment is the Tornado Air-defense aeroplane, Hawk training aeroplanes, military personnel carriers, offensive tanks, conventional arms, and other military needs. As a matter of fact, the total Saudi imports of economic and military equipment from Britain in 1979 was US$1.90 billion.[12] Moreover, there are hundreds of Saudi military personnel who received their military training in Great Britain, such as pilots, engineers, and military officers. Thus, we can say that the military relationship between Saudi Arabia and Great Britain has been a good relationship since 1979, and the two countries are working for a more positive relationship.

All in all, the relationship between Saudi Arabia, the Islamic Republic of Iran and Great Britain since 1979 is a very complicated relationship. Both countries have had their ups and downs with Great Britain. For Iran, it had a political and a diplomatic difficulty with Britain. In addition to that, it has a security problem with Britain and that is due to the British welcome of the Iranian opposition and refugees in London and other cities in Britain.

Relations with the French Republic:

The relationship between Saudi Arabia, the Islamic Republic of Iran and the French Republic since the Iranian revolution in 1979 was to be characterized as a 'Stick and Carrot' situation, particularly with the Islamic Republic of Iran. However, the relationship between Saudi Arabia and the French Republic was smooth and the two countries respected each other and there was a mutual trust in each other. The following description of the relationship is focused first on Iran and then on Saudi Arabia.

The French-Iranian relationship reached its importance when Ayatollah Khomeini was kicked out of Iraq and decided to go to Paris, the capital of France. The French government's reaction to Khomeini's decision was to send a special envoy to Tehran in order to ask Shah Mohammad Reza Pahlavi's views on the matter.[13] The Shah, in fact, did not express any opposition to Khomeini's move from Baghdad to Paris. That action gave the French government the opportunity to provide Ayatollah Khomeini with all necessary facilities and guarantee his supporters a free hand of activities in France and outside France. Ayatollah Khomeini and his supporters started to contact the people inside Iran and encourage them to move against the Shah and his government.

Moreover, Ayatollah Khomeini began from France to contact the representatives of the super powers and give interviews to journalists and reporters. Such activities made Ayatollah Khomeini accepted by many of the super powers and many of the Arabs and the Muslims all over the World. It also contributed to the fall of the Shah of Iran, who was forced to leave Tehran to the United States of America. Once the Shah left Iran, Ayatollah Khomeini left Paris to Tehran, where he was met as a hero. Automatically he announced the abolition of the monarchy and the establishment of the Islamic Republic of Iran. Ayatollah Khomeini was impressed by the French support for him and his supporters, therefore, he established very good political and commercial relations with the French.

At the same time, the number of Iranian opposition and dissidents has increased in France. Also the political organizations opposed to the Iranian Islamic Republic were created in Paris one after another. One of these organizations was called the 'National Movement of Iranian Resistance'. Shahpour Bakhtiar created it, the last Prime Minister of Iran, who was killed with his secretary by three terrorists in Paris on 8 August 1991.[14] His body was not discovered for 36 hours and the killers were able to leave France. The Foreign Minister of Iran then, Ali Akbar Velayati denied any Iranian participation in Bakhtiar's assassination. Another opposition organization was the 'Front for the Liberation of Iran'. It was established by another Prime Minister of Iran, the late Ali Amini, who died in Paris.[15] After his death, another one called 'Flag of Freedom' replaced this organization. The leader of this organization was and still is Dr. Manoutchehr Ganji, who was a University Professor and an ex-Minister of Education.[16] In fact, this organization was the most active organization among the others. It has many contacts inside and outside Iran and its headquarter is in Paris.

With regard to the French government, it expected a big reward from the Islamic regime in Iran because of its support for Ayatollah Khomeini and his supporters, but it was disappointed. When the Iraq-Iran War started in 1980, France had 40,000 refugees from Iran, and she was contractually obliged to sell arms to Iraq. This fact changed Iran's view of the French Republic, and she began its terrorist operations inside France, particularly against the Iranian opposition and dissidents. France was looking at the War between Iraq and Iran with a very realistic vision. It was very clear, at the time, that if Iraq is defeated in that War, the whole Arabian/Persian Gulf region will suffer. However, the war was ended with neither a winner nor a loser, and the Arabian/Persian Gulf region took a deep breath.

At the end of the War, Iran needed to borrow billions of dollars to reconstruct its infrastructure and to repair the ruins of the war. France was ready to give a good amount of credits and she did not spare any effort to help Iran. Therefore, the economic and financial ties between the two countries were developed and prospered. This fact has made France change its policies toward the Iranian opposition where it started tightening on their activities inside France. Thus, the Iranian opposition inside France has suffered from the French position and one by one they had to cease their activities in Paris. Some of the Iranian opposition elements decided to go to Iraq and either work independently or join the Mujahideen Khalq organization.[17]

On the economic side, France has stood against the American economic embargo of Iran along with the European Union and objected strongly to the American decision. This French position has encouraged some of European companies dealing in oil to invest in Iran. Among these companies are the French oil company 'TOTAL' which signed in 1997, a US$2 billion oil contract, which was considered as the biggest oil contract, and 'ELF' oil company, which has signed a US$1.3 billion contract for improving oil wells in the Southern part of Iran. In fact, French oil companies are investing and working freely in Iran. They are exploiting Iranian oil resources. At the same time, Alsthom Company, which is specialized in airways maintenance, has signed also a contract to repair and complete the Iranian Airways. In fact, Iranian Airways is planning to purchase a fleet of Airbus aeroplanes from France.[18] In addition, Iran is importing spare-parts, machines, raw materials, and other goods and materials from France.

In addition to the above-mentioned relations with France, the Islamic Republic of Iran has established intelligence and security offices inside France. These offices were given instructions to perform the following tasks:

(1) collecting political and military information.

(2) collecting economic and social information.

(3) gathering people and holding seminars.

(4) assassinating opposition elements.[19]

(5) collecting information on Iranian dissidents and refugees.[20]

Thus, the people who were in charge of these offices knew in advance their targets and goals and were very punctual in implementing them. Some of them were military personnel and some of them were intelligence officers. Nevertheless, they were very loyal to the Iranian regime and we have not seen any deserter or a refuge from them. As a matter of fact, they were chosen and selected very carefully by the Iranian regime.

In the cultural field, there is a cultural agreement between Iran and France that was signed in the late 1950s. This cultural agreement gives the right to Iran to establish Persian schools in France and France will have the right to establish French schools in Iran. Other items were also included in the agreement.

With regard to the Saudi-French relationship, it was and still is a very positive relationship, but not without some handicaps and some negatives. For example, during the tripartite attack on Egypt in 1956, France had participated in that attack along with England and Israel. The Saudi reaction was very strong and Saudi Arabia severed its diplomatic relationship with France after condemning the attack on Egypt. Historically, this was the first modern or contemporary misunderstanding between the two countries. However, during the 1967 Arab-Israeli war, France condemned the Israeli attack on Arabs and called for the withdrawal of Israeli forces from the occupied Arab land. The same thing happened during the 1973 Arab-Israeli war when France contributed to the cease fire of the warring parties and called for peaceful talks between the warring factions. Nevertheless, it seems that France has learned the lesson from its attack on Egypt in 1956.

Moreover, the Kingdom of Saudi Arabia has been supportive of the countries that were under the colonization of the Western powers in Africa and Asia. Therefore, it has given full support to Algeria to be independent from the French colonization in 1962. This Saudi position, however, created another misunderstanding between the two countries and particularly France put the relationship between them on hold.

With regard to the religious relationship between the two countries, France is a secular country, and practicing of religion is free for everybody including the French people. In fact, there are approximately one million persons (1,000,000) of French nationality who believe and practice Islam as a religion. In the mean time, there are approximately four million persons (4,000,000) from the Arab and non-Arab Muslims who believe in Islam and practice it as a religion in France. Due to these facts, there are many mosques around France. In fact, there are six major mosques all over France. The main two mosques that are allocated inside Paris, the French capital, are called the 'Babri' Mosque and the 'Da'wah' Mosque.[21] French and non-French Muslims visit Saudi Arabia to perform Umrah (the Lesser Hajj) and to perform Hajj (the Great Hajj).[22] Beside that, there is a cultural agreement which was signed between the two countries in the early 1960s and both countries respect the culture and tradition of each other.

On the other hand, the security relationship between the two countries goes back to the 1970s. Both countries have established a sound relationship through their Ministries of Interior. That relationship was spread in 1975 to the two countries Intelligence Services. Nevertheless, in the same year, 1975, the two countries decided to establish a secret club called the 'Safari Club' for fighting 'Communism'. Later, they were joined by Egypt, Iran, and Morocco.[23] That club was to continue until the fall of Shah Mohammad Reza Pahlavi in 1979. There was also cooperation between the two Ministries of Interior. They exchanged information regarding terrorism and other security matters. Both sides exchanged visits of experts and had good ties concerning bilateral security issues.

In the military field, the relationship between Saudi Arabia and France goes back to the 1960s. The Kingdom imports a number of military hardware. However, the major cooperation between the two countries is in the field of navy ships and navy equipment. Nowadays, Saudi Arabia imports the spare parts for the navy ships that it bought from France. In the meantime, there was a serious negotiation between the two countries indicating that Saudi Arabia was willing to buy 300 tanks of 'Le Klark' type. The total value of the deal was US$3.5 billion.[24] There was also an exchange of visits between the military experts of the two countries including the bilateral visits between the two Ministers of Defense.

With regard to the economic relationship between France and Saudi Arabia, the Kingdom imports all kinds of commodities that were manufactured in France. These imports included cars, televisions, ovens, refrigerators, furniture, textiles and other French manufactured items. France, on the other hand, imports oil from Saudi Arabia and has an interest in investing into Saudi oil fields. Besides that, France has many companies that are working in Saudi Arabia. These included construction companies, telecommunication companies, and machinery companies. Moreover, there was an airway agreement between the two countries. According to that agreement, Saudi Arabian Airlines could fly twice a week between Riyadh and Jeddah airports to Paris Charles De Gaul airport. Air France, on the other hand, could fly twice a week between Charles De Gaul airport to Riyadh and Jeddah airports. An additional flight to and from Dammam airport occasionally took place. During Hajj time there are special Hajj flights from both sides.

In addition, there was a French-Saudi Friendship Society established in 1989, headed by Mr. Herve De Charette. He had two vice presidents. The Society's goals were as follows:

a) **to promote the political, economic, and social life of the two countries.**

b) **to enhance the friendly relationship between the two countries.**

c) **to encourage trade and business between the two countries.**

d) **to encourage bilateral visits of political and business people of the two countries.**

The society was a successful one, but it needed more encouragement and more government intervention. The Saudi side was very anxious to improve it and enhance its business. The French side was also interested in expanding the society, but was very slow and very bureaucratic.

All in all, the relationship between Saudi Arabia, Iran and France is a very good one, and the three sides need each other in developing and continuing their economic ties. Their economic relationship has been built on mutual respect and the recognition of each other's rights.

Relations with the Federal Republic of Germany:

Germany is the most important country for Iran in the European continent. Iran has a 'semi-strategic' relationship with Germany. In fact, severing its diplomatic relations with Great Britain did not harm Iran, but she was harmed when its relations with Germany witnessed some difficulties. Therefore, she wanted always to keep good relations with Germany for a number of reasons:

(a) historically, Iran was an ally of Germany during its Second World War, and the Germans had an open tendency towards the Iranians. In the past, while both the Russians and the British wanted to humiliate and defeat the Iranians, the Germans had a favorable feeling towards the Iranians.

(b) economically, Iran was dependent on Germany for supplying its markets with different commercial items that are manufactured in Germany. In the mean time, she was in need of German financial assistance. The Germans also built roads and established German Banks in Tehran and other cities.[25]

(c) politically, Iran was in need of Germany to break its isolation especially in Europe. As a matter of fact, in the post World War II period, the two countries in 1955 promoted their consulates to embassy status, and reconfirmed their bilateral treaties.[26]

(d) culturally, there are historical cultural ties between the two countries, which were started in 1899. In fact, a German school for teaching the German language was opened in 1907. According to a statistics that was run in 1976, there were more than one thousand students in that school. In the mean time, it was Germany, which established the Iranian Broadcasting System in Tehran in the late 1930s.[27]

(e) the existence of a number of treaties like the treaty of friendship, the treaty of commerce, which was signed first in 1857. In 1954, this commercial treaty was reconfirmed and a technical section was added to it.[28]

The most important event, which harmed this very close relationship, and the event that 'broke the camel's back' was the 'Myconos' terrorist incident, which happened on 17 September 1992. That incident which took place in Berlin, cost the life of four Iranian-Kurdish opposition members, among them was the leader of the Democratic Kurdish Party (KDP). The reaction of the German government was very quick and it accused the Iranian government of supporting this terrorist incident. The German government also had sent off four Iranian diplomats and had arrested four Lebanese citizens and one Iranian citizen. The investigation of the incident proved, after four years, that Iran was involved and that President Hashemi Rafsanjani and his chief of Intelligence Mr. Ali Falahiyan had given the order to carry out the terrorist operation.[29] This terrorist act happened despite the fact that Iran had an intelligence relationship with the German Intelligence Organization (BND).

As far as Saudi Arabia's relations with the German Republic, that relationship was, historically, not good. However, their relationship started first in 1929 when King Abd Al-Aziz signed the friendship treaty with Germany. In 1938, the German Ambassador to Baghdad was appointed as the first non-resident Ambassador to Saudi Arabia. During the Second World War, Saudi Arabia allied itself with the Allied European forces against the Germans. In the mean time, there was a good deal of commercial relationship between the two countries, especially with the Hijaz region, now known as the Western Province. In 1954, Saudi Arabia started again a sound diplomatic, political and commercial relationship with Western Germany. Due to the fact that Eastern Germany was categorized as a communist country, Saudi Arabia never had a diplomatic or a commercial relationship with it. Nevertheless, the relationship between the two countries was to end in 1964 as a result of Germany's establishing a diplomatic and a political relationship with Israel. In 1973, the relationship was to resume again.

On the other hand, there were a number of political visits between the two countries on a high level. Among those visits are the following:[30]

(1) the visit of the German chancellor to Riyadh in 1976.

(2) the visit of the Crown Prince of Saudi Arabia Prince Fahd Bin Abd Al-Aziz to Bonn and Berlin in 1978.

(3) the visit of King Khalid Bin Abd Al-Aziz to Bonn in 1980.

(4) the visit of Chancellor Kohl to Riyadh in 1985.

(5) the visit of Prince Saud Al-Faisal, the Saudi Foreign Minister to Bonn in October 1990.

In addition to these visits, there was an agreement, which was signed between the Gulf Cooperation Council (GCC) and the European Union in 15 June 1988, when the German Republic became the President of the European Union (EU) and Saudi Arabia became the President of GCC.[31]

Concerning the economic relationship between the two countries, there were old commercial ties between the Hijaz region and Germany. After the establishment of the Kingdom of Saudi Arabia in 1932, and the discovery of oil, these ties grew and the Kingdom became one of the largest markets for German products in the Middle East region. For example, the Kingdom imports from Germany several items such as air conditions, cars, refrigerators, kitchen materials, and furniture. In addition, there is a Saudi-German economic committee, which was established in 1985.[32] This committee is to focus on encouraging companies from the private sector and the public sector to invest in Germany and in Saudi Arabia. As a matter of fact, during the late 1970s and 1980s, there were 71 Saudi/German companies, 36 of them were in the manufacturing sector and the rest in the trade sector. In 1996, the two countries signed an economic treaty, which was to focus on German investment in Saudi Arabia. The committee also focused on joint ventures, particularly in a third country.[33] In the meantime, the committee meets once a year, one year in Berlin, and the other year in Riyadh. In fact, the German companies have built the major airports in Saudi Arabia, including the King Khalid airport in Riyadh. They have also built the main highways in the Kingdom, and a huge sports stadium in Riyadh.

Regarding the religious relationship between the two countries, there is in fact official German recognition of Islam, and the German government was considering recognising Islam as a religion in Germany. However, Islam was attracting the German youth, as some 300 German citizens became Muslims every year.[34] The number of Turkish Muslim citizens in Germany is approximately 2.3 million as of 1996. Other Muslims were about 200,000 of different Arab and non-

Arab nationalities. There were a number of Islamic centers in different German cities, such as the Hamburg Islamic Center, and the small Islamic centers in Berlin. There were also several mosques all around Germany, and there was a plan to build a huge mosque in Berlin to accommodate about ten thousand (10,000) people.(35) In 1993 the Berlin Municipality gave the order to build this mosque. In addition, there were a number of Islamic associations in Germany such as in Berlin, Hamburg, and Duesseldorf.   Saudi Arabia had religious relationships with these Islamic centers and associations, which are receiving copies of the Quran, which is printed in King Fahd's Complex for Printing the Holy Quran in Al-Madinah.   They also received Islamic books and financial assistance from the Kingdom of Saudi Arabia.

Culturally speaking, there is a cultural agreement between the two countries, which was signed in 1987 between the Ministers of Foreign Affairs of the two States.   In fact, there were 150 Saudi students studying medicine in Germany in 1980, and there was a Saudi cultural office there.   In the 1970s and the 1980s there were more than a thousand students in Germany, most studying medicine and other scientific subjects.   Moreover, there were a number of agreements between the Saudi Universities and the German Universities.   In addition, there were a number of German teachers who taught the German language in King Abd Al-Aziz University in Jeddah, and King Saud University in Riyadh. The German embassy in Riyadh and the German Consulate in Jeddah offered evening classes for the Saudis who would like to study the German language.(36)

There was also a growing information exchange between the two countries.   There were also a number of German journalists who visited Saudi Arabia and wrote about its international and local politics, economies, and social development. In addition, there were a number of Saudi exhibits in Germany such as the exhibit of 'Riyadh Between Yesterday and Today' which was shown in three German cities.   The exhibit of 'Jubail and Yanbu', which was shown in Bonn, beside the exhibit of the 'Saudi Lady Artists of Painting'.(37)   Besides that, the Saudi offices in Germany provided a German-Arabic speaking program with the Kingdom's news and developments in the country.

Militarily speaking, the Kingdom has purchased, since the early 1980s, a number of military items from Germany.   These items include armored personnel carriers, type 'Fox', light missile launchers, and spare parts.

In conclusion, the relationship between Saudi Arabia, Iran and Western Germany was still a good relationship despite some difficulties, particularly between Iran and Western Germany. Western Germany knows the importance of the two countries (Saudi Arabia and Iran) in the Middle East. She knows their importance as oil exporting countries, and she knows their political and economic weight in the region, particularly in the oil field. Nonetheless, their relationship is built on mutual respect and mutual interests. In the mean time, all parties know that their bilateral relationship is very important in the international arena. Therefore, each party was keen to maintain good relations with the other.

CONCLUSION:

The relationship between Saudi Arabia, the Islamic Republic of Iran and Western Europe is an interesting relationship. Yes, it is built on a very complicated base, and it has some ups and downs, but the two countries, i.e. Saudi Arabia and The Islamic Republic of Iran, know the political, economic, and military importance of Western Europe. They know its political weight internationally. They also know its weight in the international organizations and in the government and non-government organizations. In fact, Western Europe is considered as the backbone of Saudi Arabia and Iran. Geographically speaking, Saudi Arabia and Iran are located in a very strategic area in the Arabian/Persian Gulf region. They both have oil reserves that will last for more than one hundred years, for Saudi Arabia, and for more than fifty years for the Islamic Republic of Iran. The Western World, in general, needs the oil of the two countries, and also needs their markets.

Both Saudi Arabia and the Islamic Republic of Iran have security and intelligence relationships with most of the countries of Western Europe. They exchange security and intelligence information on a regular basis. They also exchange expert visits on an annual basis. A training program is also conducted between the intelligence services of some of the Western countries and Saudi Arabia in the field of intelligence. This shows that the Western countries have a stronger belief in Saudi Arabia than in the Islamic Republic of Iran.

Historically speaking, the major powers in Western Europe such as Great Britain, France, and Germany, know the importance of both Saudi Arabia and the Islamic Republic of Iran. They and other countries in Western Europe want to get closer to them and have a very close relationship with them. Moreover, understanding that the policies of Saudi Arabia and the Islamic Republic of Iran affect their interests in the Arabian/Persian Gulf region, most of the Western European countries would approach the two countries with careful strategic policies. For example, the Federal Republic of Germany had to tolerate the Iranian policies through out the 1980s and the 1990s and become a patient country. France had also the same problem with the Islamic Republic of Iran particularly in the security field.

Saudi Arabia on the other hand, has had a smooth relationship with Western Europe, except the historical background between Saudi Arabia and Germany in 1940, and Great Britain and France in 1956. After World War II, the relationship between Saudi Arabia and the major powers of Europe went very smoothly and covered all aspects of life. Their mutual interests were served by this relationship and their respect for each other was increasing day by day.

Finally, despite the ups and downs in their historical and current relationship, all countries in Western Europe wanted to have a good and lasting relationship with both Saudi Arabia and the Islamic Republic of Iran. They were tolerant with Iran and its policies and very nice with Saudi Arabia and its policies too.

FOOTNOTES

(1) Majed Omer, 'Al-Ittihad' Newspaper, No.8803, June,15,1999.

(2) Dr. Mohammad Hassan Al-Aidarous, 'The Arab/Iranian Relations', Dar Al-Kitab Al-Hadeeth. P110

(3) Ibid. pp.53-55.

(4) Ibid. pp.162-166.

(5) This diplomatic situation did not change until 1999, when the two countries agreed to upgrade the diplomatic representation in both countries, and they sent ambassadors to each other's capitals.

(6) 'Al-Moujez- an-Iran', Vol. 9,No.2, October, 1999. P.16

(7) Ibid.

(8) Ibid.

(9) Ibid. p.17

(10) Mohammad El-Mas'ari is a political dissident who escaped from Saudi Arabia to Britain. In London, he waged a political war against the Kingdom of Saudi Arabia. Osama Faqih was the right hand of El-Mas'ari and his financial assistant. In fact, Faqih was the brain of El-Mas'ari and his mastermind. Recently, the two have had a quarrel and have spilt.

(11) Gulf States Newsletter, West Sussex, United Kingdom, No. 371, October,2,1989, P.16.

(12) William B. Quant, 'Saudi Arabia in the 1980s, Foreign Policy, Security, and Oil'. The Brookings Institution, October,1981, P.162.

(13) A special interview with an Iranian opposition leader who lives in France and who did not want his name to be mentioned. The interview took place in Paris on February, 14, 1989.

(14) Shahpour Bakhtiar was killed in his home in Paris on August, 8, 1991. He was killed by terrorists sent by the Islamic regime in Iran. They were able to flee the country and go back to Iran. The Islamic regime in Iran denied the charges.

(15) Ali Amini was a very famous figure in Iran. He was appointed as Prime Minister of Iran by Shah Mohammad Reza Pahlavi in the 1970s.

(16) Dr. Manouchehr Ganji is a respectable man who wanted to free Iran from the hands of the Mullahs and establish a Republican

regime where politics is separated from religion.

(17) The Mujahideen Khalq Organization is a major opposition group working against the Islamic Republic regime in Iran. It is supported by Iraq and has a major headquarter inside Baghdad. It is still active and wages military attacks against Iran from the Iraqi border.

(18) A special interview with an Iranian opposition leader who lives in France, Februray,14,1989.

(19) France is considered as the safe haven for Iranian murderers. No murderer has been hung by the French authorities, even if he is 100% guilty. For example, when Dr. Reza Mazluman (known as Aryamansh) was assassinated in Germany, his assassin was Ahmed Gihouni, who lived in Germany for 12 years under a commercial cover. He was captured by the French authorities and put in prison.

(20) There are one million Iranian dissidents and refugees in Europe. However, they are not recognized, in many of the European countries, as refugees.

(21) There is a misunderstanding and a quarrel between the Arab Muslims on who should have control over the mosques' affairs. The Algerians are fighting with the Saudis and the Saudis are fighting with the Turks on who should become the Imam of the different mosques. However, and for the time being, the Algerians are running the 'Babri' mosque and the Imam of the mosque is an Algerian Muslim.

(22) The Umrah is called the Lesser Hajj because it could be performed all year around and without visiting Arafat, Muzdalifah, and Mena, which are considered as the holy shrines of the Great Hajj. The Great Hajj, however, is performed once a year and only the financially able Muslim is required to perform the Great Hajj once in a lifetime. Nevertheless, there are 1.9 million who performed Greater Hajj in 2000. See also Saudi Press Agency (SPA), dated 03/10/2000.

(23) For more details on the 'Safari Club', Please read Saeed M. Badeeb, 'Saudi-Iranian Relations(1932-1982)', Center for Arab-Iranian Studies and Echoes, London 1993. P.65.

(24) Saudi Arabia is putting one condition on France and that is to invest 37% of the value of the deal in the local industry of the Kingdom. In fact, the Kingdom wants to imitate the same system that it has with the British on the 'Yamamah' project.

(25) When the Iran-Iraq war was over in 1988, Iran had no outside debt. Nowadays, Iran is in debt for more than US$30 billion. To

Germany alone, Iran is in debt for US$20 billion.

(26) DAD, German Exchange of Academic Stuff, (February, 1988,) pp.364-373

(27) Ibid. p.367

(28) Ibid.

(29) The 'Myconos' incident was a big terrorist operation. It took place in a restaurant called 'Myconos' in Berlin, West Germany. The Iranian opposition groups used to gather and dine in that restaurant.

(30) Mohammad Hassan Yaf'i, 'The Federal Republic of Germany and the Bilateral Relations with the Kingdom of Saudi Arabia', Bonn, 1991, pp.72-73

(31) Ibid. P.73

(32) Ibid. P.75

(33) Ibid. P.76

(34) See 'Ahdath Al-Alem Al-Islami', (Events of the Islamic World) in 1999, The International Islamic News Agency, (EENA), p.353.

(35) Ibid. p.354

(36) Mohammad Hassan Yaf'i, PP.78-79.

(37) Ibid. pp.80-81.

CHAPTER FOUR

SAUDI ARABIA, IRAN AND THE UNITED STATES

As we have seen, the relations between Saudi Arabia and the Islamic Republic of Iran have been problematic, ranging from antagonism to coexistence but rarely cordial. At first glance, that might seem strange, given the similarities between the two countries. Both societies are Muslim and both governments are based on Islamic legal principles, albeit the Saudi regime is monarchical and Sunni and the Iranian regime is republican and Shiite. Ironically, although both regimes denounced atheistic communism, relations were worse prior to the end of the Cold War in the 1980s than subsequently.

One way to assess the reasons for the lack of cordiality between the two countries is to look at how they view the world around them, particularly the state of their relations with the one remaining superpower, the United States. Relations among Saudi Arabia, Iran and the United States go back to the 1930s and were initially built on mutual respect and mutual recognition of security, oil and economic interests, and in the case of Saudi Arabia and Iran, on peaceful coexistence.

In order to analyse this three-way relationship, we need to look at several questions, which represent its most important aspects: What is the historical impact on the relationship? What is the political basis for the relationship? What is the economic basis for the relationship? And what is the military background for this relationship? This chapter will focus on these four basic aspects of both bilateral and trilateral relations.

Saudi Arabia and the United States

Historical Background:

Saudi bilateral relations with the United States began in 1933 when and American oil company, Standard Oil of California applied for and received a concession agreement to explore for oil.[1] King Abd Al-Aziz had granted an earlier concession to a British company but it failed to find oil. Moreover, the King felt more comfortable with an American company because the United States had no colonial interests in Arabia. Indeed, in the early years, the relationship was commercial rather than diplomatic as the Kingdom dealt directly with the oil company, California Arabian Standard Oil Company (CASOC), the ancestor of Saudi Aramco.

The company struck oil in 1935 but did not discover it in commercial quantities until 1938. Because of the deteriorating international situation leading to World War II, it was not able to export the oil. Because of the international situation, the Kingdom was also hurting economically because its chief source of income, receipts of Hajjis, Muslim pilgrims to Makkah and Al-Madinah, had fallen drastically as the clouds of war spread through the Muslim World. Finally, the United States signed a Lend Lease agreement with the Kingdom to keep it economically viable during the war years. It was not until 1945 that oil exports began, transforming Saudi Arabia into the modern oil Kingdom it is today.

The first American diplomatic mission to Saudi Arabia was established in 1942 when a permanent chargè d'affaires established a legation in Jeddah. Two years later, in 1944, the first Saudi diplomatic mission was opened in Washington D.C. Soon thereafter, both missions were raised to the status of Embassy with resident ambassadors.

On February 14,1945, a meeting took place between King Abd Al-Aziz and President Franklin Roosevelt in the Suez Canal, on board the USS Quincy. It was the first official meeting of heads of state of the two countries. This historic meeting cemented political relations between Saudi Arabia and the United States whose relations had previously been largely limited to petroleum commerce. Recognizing the global importance of Saudi oil, and the global security importance of the United States as the military leader of the allied forces against Germany and Japan in World War II, it paved the way to close cooperation between Saudi Arabia and the United States in what was to evolve as a 'strategic relationship'.[2] This strategic relationship has combined a number of aspects ranging between political, economic, and military relationship.

Over the years that followed, there have been many chief of state meetings, all reaffirming the close ties between the two countries. On January 30, 1957, King Saud Ibn Abd Al-Aziz visited Washington, where he met with President Dwight D. Eisenhower. His majesty also paid another visit to Washington in 1962 where he met with President John F. Kennedy.[3] His successor, King Faisal Ibn Abd Al-Aziz, paid two state visits to the United States. The first was in June 1966 when he met with President Lyndon Johnson. He paid a second state visit in 1971, where he met with President Richard Nixon. Prior to becoming King, then Prince Faisal paid two official visits to the United States as Foreign Minister. The first visit was in the fall of 1943 and the second visit was in February 1944 when he represented Saudi Arabia in signing the agreement to establish the United Nations in San Francisco.[4] King Faisal was the most experienced Saudi leader in foreign affairs, having held the position of Foreign Minister from its creation until his death in 1975.

His brother, King Khalid Ibn Abd Al-Aziz who made a state visit to Washington in 1977 where he met with President Jimmy Carter, succeeded King Faisal. The following year, 1978, President Carter responded by coming to Saudi Arabia, meeting with King Khalid and then Crown Prince Fahd.

All the visits of King Faisal were official events in which there were several accomplishments. On the other hand His Majesty King Khalid Ibn Abd Al-Aziz came to Washington in 1977. He met with President Jimmy Carter on that visit. In 1978, President Jimmy Carter arrived in Saudi Arabia to meet with King Khalid and then Crown Prince Fahd Ibn Abd Al-Aziz. King Fahd had made four official visits to the United States before becoming King: in 1944 when the United Nations was established, in 1945 at the first meeting of the United Nations, in 1974 when he signed the agreement for the Saudi-American Joint Economic Commission, and in 1977 when he met with President Jimmy Carter. His last visit, as King, was in February 1985 when he met with President Ronald Reagan.[5] The continuity of these visits has enabled the two countries to maintain close and cordial relations over the years in political, security and economic affairs.

The success of the two countries to work together in mutual harmony and respect does not mean that the relationship has been without strains. The greatest strain has been over the dispossession of the Palestinians from their homeland by the creation of the state of Israel and the noticeable reluctance on the part of the United States to incur domestic political costs at home to use its overwhelming influence to bring about a just and lasting peace. The US record has been uneven. Despite President Roosevelt's promise to King Abd Al-Aziz that the United States would consult with him and other Arabs in the resolution of the Palestinian conflict, it did not do so while engineering the dispossession of the Arabs and the creation of Israel in 1947-1948.

The American record was somewhat more even-handed in 1956 when Great Britain, France, and Israel invaded Egypt in retaliation for the nationalization of the Suez Canal by President Jamal Abd Al-Nasser. This attack, called 'The Tripartite Attack', was condemned by Saudi Arabia, which demanded a cease fire and the intervention of the United States to force the occupying forces to withdraw from Egyptian territory. In the beginning, the United States was reluctant, but with strong political pressure by the Saudis and threats from the Soviet Union, the United States intervened and forced the three countries to cease their attack. It was a crucial moment for both the Americans and the Saudis.

In June 1967, a second Arab-Israeli war erupted when Israel launched a pre-emptive strike against all its Arab neighbours. In response to the United States all-out support of Israel, Saudi Arabia reacted by levying an oil embargo against the United States and Western European countries. The embargo was not effective due to the world glut of oil, but relations between Saudi Arabia and the United States suffered a setback.

A third Arab-Israeli war broke out in 1973 when President Sadat invaded the Sinai Peninsula, under Israeli military occupation since 1967. In this case, King Faisal felt personally betrayed when the Americans hastily replaced heavy Israeli losses in aircraft and weapons and announced a multi-billion dollar military aid package to Israel, despite the fact that President Nixon had personally promised the King that the United States would remain even-handed. The Saudis had no choice but to levy another oil embargo against the United States and its allies. Because of a world shortage in oil, it was very effective and the United States, failing to remember the Saudi resolve in 1967, were forced to take into account the effect of their actions in support of Israel on the Arab World generally.

One can only conclude that one-sided US support for Israel has been a major obstacle to otherwise cordial relations between the United States and Saudi Arabia for the half-century and more. The strain in the relationship has been in proportion to the degree to which the United States has supported Israel against the Palestinians and Arabs in general.

Recent Saudi-American Relations:

Over the past sixty years, relations between Saudi Arabia and the United States of America have evolved steadily in all fields, including foreign policy and diplomacy, national security and military cooperation, commerce and trade, education, and health. At times one and then another took priority.

Military Relations:

Beginning in the late 1940s, the spread of atheistic communist doctrines by the Soviet Union threatened the Islamic character of the entire Middle East region. In order to counter that threat, Saudi Arabia looked to the United States to help it create a new, modern military force. The United States also constructed an air base at Dhahran and in return was allowed to use it to counter the Soviet threat. That began a military relationship that has lasted to the present day.

In the 1960s, a wave of socialist Arab nationalism engulfed much of the Middle East, led by Egypt's President Jamal Abd Al-Nasser. With the encouragement of the Soviet Union, Egyptian troops were sent to North Yemen to prop up the republican regime that had overthrown the traditional Islamic Imamate. This expansion of Soviet influence was not only a threat to Saudi Arabia but to the entire region. The Kingdom and the United States developed, in endeavouring to counter the threat, a close 'Strategic Relationship' in the sense that the security and stability of the Kingdom became very important for the United States, and the two countries have worked very hard to cooperate with each other to preserve that relationship.

On August 2, 1990, military relations became the main focus as

Iraq invaded Kuwait and the two countries were dragged into a serious war against Iraq. Saudi-American military relations were long-standing as the United States aided the Kingdom in creating, training and equipping of a modern military force and a United States military presence in the region was seen as a major deterrent to potential regional confrontations, but direct American combat involvement in the region was not foreseen.

Saudi Arabia and a number of the Arab-Gulf countries, including Kuwait, had supported Iraq in its eight year war with the Islamic Republic of Iran, i.e. from 1980 to 1988.[6] The war between Iraq and Iran was a critical strategic importance, involving two major oil exporting countries that share a long land and river border. It pitted Arab against Persian and a Sunni government in Baghdad against a Shi'ite government in Tehran, but it also involved Iraqi Shi'ites against Iranian Shi'ites.[7] For Iraq to turn around and invade Kuwait and threaten Saudi Arabia, was therefore a treacherous act. Following the invasion of Kuwait, Iraqi President Saddam Hussein signed an agreement with Iran in which he withdrew his forces and troops from the Iranian occupied land and agreed to adhere to the terms of an earlier first agreement with Iran which he had signed in Algeria.

Iraq had never wholly given up its claim to Kuwait, dating back to the time when it was under the Ottoman province of Basrah prior to World War I. Following the war, the British joined Basrah and Mosul in the North to Baghdad to create Iraq, but did not include Kuwait. From time to time, Iraqis raised their claim, but prior to the invasion, had never backed it up with force.

The immediate issue leading to the 1990 invasion was oil rights. Iraq accused Kuwait of drilling horizontally into Iraqi oil from wells near the border. The Kuwaitis denied the accusation and the two countries met in Jeddah, Saudi Arabia, on 1 August, ostensibly to negotiate a settlement under Saudi mediation.

The Saudis could not get the two parties to agree on anything, including oil policies, modification of the borders, and the Kuwaiti financial aid to Iraq.[8] The next day, Iraq launched a full scale invasion. The invasion constituted blatant aggression and threatened all the Arab oil producing states in the Arabian Peninsula. Diplomatic efforts from all over the world sought to convince Saddam Hussein to withdraw his troops from Kuwait, but to no avail. Therefore, Saudi Arabia had no choice but to invite Arab, Muslim, European and

American troops to the region to eject him by force.

In hindsight, it does not appear that Saddam Hussein had any intention of reaching a settlement. On the contrary, he appears to have been implementing the first step of a 'grand design' for placing the entire region under Iraqi hegemony. This scenario entailed invading Kuwait first, then occupying the Eastern Province of Saudi Arabia, giving him 45 percent of the world's oil. Finally he would encourage his partners in the Arab Cooperation Council (ACC), Jordan and Yemen, to attack Saudi Arabia from the south, parts of which San'a still claimed, and the northwestern, for the Hashimites to regain the Hijaz which they once ruled. This would leave the Royal family of Saudi Arabia with only the Najd region of central Arabia. Saddam Hussein would gain full control of Kuwait and the Eastern part of Saudi Arabia, giving him virtual control over the international oil market.

The Saudis became aware of this scenario in the first few days of Iraq's occupation of Kuwait and responded by supporting coalition efforts to force Iraqi troops out of Kuwait. Saddam further showed his intentions by seeking to intimidate other Gulf States. The Minister of Foreign Affairs of the United Arab Emirates acknowledged that Saddam was concurrently seeking to bend the UAE to his will:

'...the United Arab Emirates has received a warning message from Saddam Hussein in July 1990 threatening the UAE and demanding a sharp rise in oil prices.[9]

When it became apparent that Saddam Hussein would not yield to international pressure and withdraw his forces from Kuwait, the United States and the other coalition partners initiated Desert Storm beginning with a massive air attack against the Iraqi forces in Kuwait on 15 February 1991. In less than three days, they fled from Kuwait and Saddam Hussein was forced to sign a cease fire agreement. [10]

On balance, the Gulf war to oust Iraqi troops from Kuwait greatly strengthened military ties between Saudi Arabia and the United States. The American response showed that the United States was truly committed to the regional security and stability of the Gulf region, and that Saudi Arabia was fully prepared to cooperate toward those ends. The enhanced mutual understanding was a sound basis for their continued cooperation.

Political and Economic Relations:

Saudi-American political and economic relations evolved together. From one of the poorest countries on earth, Saudi Arabia evolved into a wealthy oil power by the 1970s. In its new role, it has developed a partnership with the United States in seeking peaceful settlement of regional conflicts and evolutionary change rather than destructive revolutionary change in the Middle East.

Political relations actually began after economic relations. American oil companies pioneered the latter in the 1930s that created what ultimately became the Arabian American Oil Company (Aramco) and subsequently the wholly Saudi-owned Saudi Aramco of today. It was not until the 1940s, during World War II, that formal diplomatic relations between the two countries were established. At that time, Saudi Arabia was virtually the only fully independent State in the Arab World. From the start, political relations were built on mutual interests, mutual understanding, and mutual respect.

In 1973, Saudi Arabia became a major oil power to reckon with, having over one fourth of the world's proved oil reserves. Concerned that relations with a country of such strategic importance had suffered as a result of the Arab oil embargo, the United States decided to establish 'a special relationship' with Saudi Arabia and seek more stability and security in that desert country.[11]

During King Khalid's rule (1975-1982), Saudi relations with the United States continued to be strengthened. With increased oil revenues, the Kingdom invited many US companies to participate in its economic development plans as well as its military modernization programs, including aircraft, radars, construction and expansion of military bases around the Kingdom. Moreover, the level of political relations also improved as the Kingdom attempted to become a moderating influence in Middle East politics. This cooperation has continued under King Fahd as the Saudi-American political relationship, now over a half-century-old, has matured with mutual understanding and respect.

From the first days of American oil concession in the Kingdom, after a British concession failed to discover oil exploration, Saudi Arabia has enjoyed excellent economic relations with the United States. In 1938, the Americans found oil in commercial quantities in the Eastern Province of Saudi Arabia, but due to the beginning of World War II, oil was not produced until 1943 when Saudi Arabia had extended its oil agreement with the United States.[12] In the 1970s, the Kingdom instituted a policy of gradually buying out American equity in Aramco until it became a wholly owned Saudi state company.

Saudi Arabia's gaining control of its national oil assets was underscored during the October 1973 Arab-Israeli conflict, when Saudi Arabia led the Arab oil embargo. Although Saudi-American relations suffered, it forced the United States and other major oil consuming countries to realize that economic well being in the Middle East was tied to political well being in seeking a peaceful settlement that afforded basic justice to the dispossessed Palestinians. It also has attracted their attention to the importance of Saudi Arabia as an oil exporting country.[13]

Saudi Arabia, which produces over eight million barrels of crude oil a day, is now the world's largest exporter of oil. It is likely to remain the leading oil producer/exporter well into the 22nd century, and is only now beginning to develop its large natural gas fields. It also has other mineral resources, including phosphates and gold, making the Kingdom one of the richest countries in natural resources in the entire Middle East. Through wise leadership, the Kingdom has invested a considerable portion of its oil revenues in economic and social infrastructure projects, providing commercial opportunities for American and other firms. This in turn has expanded the economic, political and security ties between the two countries.

Security Relations:

There can be a fine line between security cooperation and interference in internal affairs. The Kingdom does not wish to interfere into the internal affairs of other countries, and at the same time it does not wish other countries to interfere in its internal affairs. Mutual respect for that principle has been the basis of security cooperation between Saudi Arabia and the United States. Consequently, there has been, since the late 1950s, close security cooperation between the two countries' law enforcement agencies, the Ministry of Interior in the Kingdom of Saudi Arabia and the United States Federal Bureau of Investigation (FBI). The two sides have dealt with some difficult and sensitive cases over the years as well as cooperating on routine matters. Difficulties have sometimes arisen over differences in the legal and judicial systems as Saudi Arabia's judicial system is based on the

Shari'a, Islamic Law, and is immutable, whereas the United States' legal system is based on Common Law, which is subject to change. Nevertheless, the two countries have worked together to transcend these differences for the common good where both have sought to understand and respect the systems of the other country.[14]

The Kingdom also developed a close intelligence sharing relationship with the United States on issues of mutual interest and concern. Intelligence cooperation began in the mid 1960s under King Faisal Ibn Abd Al-Aziz. During his reign, King Faisal authorized HE Sheikh Kamal Ibrahim Adham, an adviser at the Royal Court, to initiate secret contacts with senior officials at the US Central Intelligence Agency (CIA) and intelligence organizations of other friendly countries through the Saudi Foreign Liaison Bureau (FLB).[15] Contacts between the FLB and intelligence representatives in the Kingdom were conducted regularly. The exchange of intelligence, political and security reports, training of Saudi personnel in the Kingdom and in the United States, the exchange of bilateral visits, and other tasks were among their assigned responsibilities. Adham retired in 1980, but the contacts he initiated are still going on.

In conclusion, the relationship between Saudi Arabia and the United States of America whether it was a political relationship, or an economic relationship, or a military relationship, or a security relationship, or any other kind of relationship, was and still is a good relationship. Both countries respect the laws and rules of the other. Both countries understand that their bilateral relationship depends on mutual understanding of each other's wishes and wills. This understanding has made it possible for both countries to sign several political, economic, military, and other kinds of mutual agreements.

However, the relationship between the United States of America and the Islamic Republic of Iran was a good relationship before the Islamic Revolution of 1979. After the 1979 revolution, the relations between the two countries were cut-off. Both countries severed their diplomatic relations and their political relations were ceased. Nevertheless, the two countries are still rethinking about the resumption of their diplomatic and political relationship.

Iran and the United States

Historical Relationship:

Prior to World War II, the United States showed little interest in Iran. In the 1920s, Reza Khan Pahlavi, commander of the Persian Cossack Brigade, deposed the Qajar monarchy and had himself crowned Shah. Reza Shah, who admired autocratic government efficiency, had an affinity for Nazi Germany, which cost him his throne with the advent of the war. In 1941, Britain and the Soviet Union forced him to abdicate in favor of his son, Mohammad Reza Shah, dividing the country into spheres of influence and occupying their spheres with troops.

During the war, the United States played a major role in freeing Iran from the combined Soviet and British influence. In 1942, the young Mohammad Reza Shah Pahlavi asked the American President Roosevelt to remove the British and Soviets. Roosevelt acted immediately and arranged for the Tripartite Agreement (Iran, the Soviet Union, and the British), by which the two countries were to withdraw their troops from Iran within six months after the end of the war. In 1943, Roosevelt was able to negotiate another agreement with Premier Stalin of the Soviet Union and Prime Minister Winston Churchill of Great Britain under which the three countries would assist Iran economically and guarantee its full independence and full sovereignty over its territory.

Following the war, the Soviets tried to renege on the agreements and also insisted on an oil concession. Iran appealed to the United Nations to implement the agreements, and with US support the Soviets were forced to withdraw their troops, enabling Iran to regain its full independence. The United States support of Iran during the war placed it in a position of great political influence in the years that followed.

During the Shah's reign, Iran occupied a special place in American Middle East policy. Not only was it a major oil producer, but also it was anti-communist and strategically located on the southern border of the Soviet Union. Moreover, its Persian population was not heavily involved in anti-Western militant Arab nationalism and antipathy toward Israel which had arisen in the Arab World after the United States had engineered the partition of Palestine, dispossessing the large Arab majority of their homeland.

When the Shah faced being deposed by a militant nationalist movement led by Mohammad Mussadeq, the United States together with the British helped engineer a pro-Shah coup to bring him back to power in 1953.[16] In the 1940s, Mussadeq tried to rise against Mohammad Reza Shah, but his attempt was suppressed. He was a strong opponent of both the monarchial rule in Iran as well as the British influence in Iran. In 1949, he created a coalition of four parties called the National Front, and in 1951, he became Prime Minister of Iran. Mussadeq quickly nationalized the British owned Anglo-Iranian Oil Company (AIOC).[17]

He calculated that by nationalizing the oil company and ousting the British, he would become a national hero and could ultimately challenge the Shah himself for power. The ploy failed when the United States sided with the British in opposing the nationalization without compensation. Mussadeq was ousted in early 1952, but was returned to power in 1953. At that point, pro-royalist forces, with the help of US and British intelligence, overthrew Mussadeq and the Shah was ushered back into power.

The Shah was still weak politically, owing the recovery of his throne to the Americans and the British, and they constituted a powerful influence in Iranian policy making. His critics charged that he was a 'stooge' of the West. The British placed an international boycott on nationalized Iranian oil, creating economic hardship until, in 1954, the Shah signed an agreement ending the oil crisis under which a consortium including British Petroleum (the successor to AIOC) and American and European oil companies took over production operations and split the profits 50-50 with Iran.[18]

The Americans were happy with their share as well as the British. As a matter of fact, it was a good reward for their role in bringing him back to power. But, on the other hand, the Shah did not want the Americans to interfere in Iranian domestic political affairs. With oil revenues again flowing in, he consolidated his personal power in Iran and ruled in an increasingly autocratic manner. He continued to depend on the Americans in the military, economic and social development fields, but not in how he ran the country. As a result, he was personally disliked by a majority of the Iranians, and his closest supporters were only those who could profit from their support.

The Americans were very much interested in developing Iran

and the Shah encouraged them to do so. In fact, they built the country's physical infrastructure from scratch, investing hundreds of millions of dollars in the country. Between 1951 and the Islamic revolution in 1979, the Americans assisted Iran in the following fields: the development of the rural areas; the development of education, health, and agriculture; the development of manufacturing and minerals; the development of water resources and the building of dams; and the development and building of roads and human resources. All these projects and programs needed a lot of money. Therefore, loans were guaranteed to Iran from the International Monetary Fund, the World Bank, and from the United States. Within twenty years, Iran became the paradise of the Middle East. Its economy was booming, its capital, Tehran, was among the most beautiful cities in the Middle East, and its agriculture was flourishing.

No doubt the Americans benefited from the presence of the Shah at the top of power in Iran. Their embassy in Tehran, opened in 1943, had become the largest American Embassy in the Middle East.[19] Iranian students were also encouraged to go to the United States to study at American universities and about 50 American universities offered assistance to various Iranian educational institutions.[20] The Shah even tolerated American Christian missionaries in Iran.

There were other reasons behind Iran's tilt towards the United States. One was the crucial US help in restoring the Shah to the Iranian throne. More importantly, however, was security. The Soviet Union had occupied parts of Iran in the recent past, and with the advent of the Cold War, had tried to create hegemony over Iran. Britain was no longer capable of defending Iran, and besides, it had also been an occupying power. The United States, as a superpower, was the only country that could protect Iran. At the same time, the United States saw Iran as the first line of defense against the Soviet Union's threat to oil producing countries and to the free flow of oil from the region to markets throughout the free world, of which the United States was the greatest oil consumer. Of course, the United States had an additional interest in protecting Iranian oil, in light of the concession agreement, which included American oil companies.[21]

The threat took on additional significance in light of the historic Russian desire to acquire a warm water port in the Gulf/Indian Ocean region. History often plays strange tricks, and the determination of the United States to defend the Gulf region from the threat of Soviet expansion is a case in point. In 1941, the United States had supplied arms to the Soviet Union through Iran.

On 20 March 1957, the Shah decided to establish a secret service, which could be of help and assistance to him. Therefore, he created SAVAK, which was established by the Central Intelligence Agency. The CIA had formed the SAVAK and used the Israeli Intelligence Service, the MOSSAD, as a partner. The SAVAK's employees had received their training from both the CIA and the MOSSAD.[22] That training was conducted inside and outside Iran.

In 1958, Iran was persuaded by the United States to enter the Central Treaty Organization (CENTO) and become a full member of that Western military alliance. Members of CENTO, which was originally the Baghdad Pact, consisted of Great Britain, Turkey, Pakistan, and, after 1958, Iran. The United States was not a formal member, not wishing to prejudice Middle East and South Asian membership with a superpower, but was closely affiliated with it. Persuading Iran to join was easy because CENTO was created as a regional security pact to counter the Soviet threat in the region in close cooperation with the North Atlantic Treaty Organization (NATO), which was established in April 1945 against the communist bloc, which established a counter organization, the Warsaw Pact, in May 1955. The Warsaw Pact was led by the Soviet Union and consisted of fourteen other Eastern European countries.

The Soviet Union was threatening the northern part of Iran since the end of World War II, therefore CENTO was a big relief for Iran, which saw it as a counter to any Soviet threat. In addition to that, it was seen as an assurance that the United States would come to its assistance if the Soviet Union or any other power threatened it militarily.

Iran signed in 1959 an Executive Agreement on Defense Cooperation. This agreement provided that the United Sates would provide assistance to Iran including arms.[23] The agreement focused on the communist threat from the Soviet Union or a client State and did not mention anything about an internal threat or a religious one. The Americans did not interfere in the internal politics of Iran or the Shah's domestic policies.

Under the agreement, Iran was able to acquire arms and munitions, military training and other material. Military relations were close, based on the mutual threat of communist expansion. The Shah also established military ties with Western European powers, but not so close as with the Americans. To strengthen the latter, he sought to establish close personal relationships with American political leaders over the years. Despite the fact that he did not want to have any American military bases in Iran, he had a military mission comprising of 25,000 Americans. This mission was comprised of troops, training personnel, maintenance personnel and military advisers. In return for his dependence on the Americans for arms, training and advice, the Shah was able to create the most powerful military force in the Gulf.

Despite their shared security and economic interests, President John F. Kennedy (1960-1963) had concerns about the increasing dictatorial nature of the Shah's regime and relations between the two countries were strained. The Shah rejected President Kennedy's criticism of his domestic policies, and maintained that Kennedy did not understand the internal problems of Iran. Following Kennedy's assassination, the Shah sent a message to President Lyndon Johnson, welcoming him as the new American president, but criticizing his predecessor for strained Iranian-American relations.[24] Nevertheless, relations between the two countries remained strained until 1970 due to the US preoccupation with the war in Vietnam and its desire not to take on any additional international problems.

Relations improved under President Richard Nixon. In 1969, he announced the Nixon Doctrine, which called for US military assistance to build up regional allies to obviate the need to send US troops, still heavily engaged in Vietnam. When the British announced their intention to end their security role in the Gulf by 1971, the United States developed a Gulf security policy based on the Nixon Doctrine called the Two Pillar Policy, which posited that Saudi Arabia and Iran would fill the 'vacuum' created by the British departure. Improved relations were reflected in the July 1972 visit of President Nixon to Iran and a return visit by the Shah to Washington in July of the following year.

The Shah envisioned Iran as the successor to Britain as the guarantor of security in the Gulf region and quickly took advantage of improved relations to try to expand his military even further, making it the largest armed force in the Gulf. Ignoring the other 'pillar', Saudi Arabia, the Shah intended to make Iran the sole 'policeman' of the

Gulf, defending it from external attack. The Shah's job was made easier by the support he had generated in the United States Congress as a front line of defense against the Soviet Union and as a non-Arab oil supplier to Israel, and the United States readily acceded to his arms requests, including F-14s for his air force.

The Arab oil embargo of 1973 brought increased oil revenues to Iran and with US willingness to sell the Shah arms, its armed forces rapidly expanded. Still, the Shah's appetite for more arms seemed insatiable. He continued to request more arms, and pushed the Organization of Petroleum Exporting Countries for ever higher prices to pay for them as well as many economic development projects. On the contrary, the United States was confident that Saudi Arabia could play an important role in protecting and defending the Gulf region.

During the energy crisis that followed the Arab oil embargo, Iran had been a leader in seeking higher prices. However, in November 1977, during a visit to Washington, the Shah was convinced by the US administration to support limiting oil price hikes. Saudi Arabia was also concerned about the negative effects of precipitous price hikes and had pushed for a pricing agreement between producers and consumers. They wanted price rises to be more gradual, linked to price rises of a basket of other commodities. Nevertheless, the Shah's decision to support limiting the rise in oil prices was appreciated by both the Saudis and the United States.

During 1978, the Shah had asked the United States for more advanced aircraft, including AWACS surveillance aircraft. The United States had always tried to respond positively to the Shah's arms requests, given the fact that Iran shared a long border with the Soviet Union, and with Congressional approval the Administration of President Jimmy Carter agreed to sell Iran the aircraft. They were never delivered, however, due to the 1979 revolution, which overthrew the Shah's regime and instituted an Islamic Republic. Despite rising domestic political unrest in Iran, Washington never anticipated that the Shah would be ousted from power. The Americans believed that he could weather the demonstrations and the riots spearheaded by students and other dissatisfied elements. Ayatollah Khomeini, who was in Paris at that time, thought otherwise and swiftly moved to consolidate his political position, convinced that the Shah would fall. He was right.

Recent Relationship:

Cordial Iranian-American relations came to an abrupt halt following the revolution. Ayatollah Khomeini returned from exile and quickly seized control of the government, instituting his own Islamic political theory which he called 'Velayat-e-Faqih', or 'governance by Islamic juridical authorities'. His hatred of Western culture, particularly that of the United States, quickly became apparent. Iran withdrew from CENTO on March 13, 1979 and abrogated all bilateral economic and defense agreements.

Khomeini began referring to the United States as 'The Great Satan' and stirring up hatred against it became a major instrument for whipping up support of the masses. The following are quotes from statements by Imam Khomeini illustrating his xenophobia:[25]

"The world should know that all the grievances of the Iranian people and the Muslim nations is because of foreigners and because of America. Whatever grievances we are facing are because of America.

"America wants you because of your oil, and because she wants to make you a market from which she will take oil and fill you with its bad goods".

Iranian foreign policy ideology during the first few years of the revolution, was based on the slogan: 'Neither the West nor the East,' shunning both the Western camp and the Eastern (communist).[26] In the Muslim World, it sought to export the Iranian revolution to Muslim countries it believed were becoming too Westernized.

The hatred of America by the Islamic regime was shown in the Iranian hostage crisis involving American diplomats in the US embassy in Tehran.[27] In November 1979, the US Embassy in Tehran was attacked and seized by Iranian students. Fifty-two American diplomats were captured and held captive for 444 days inside the embassy. They were often mistreated and some were tortured.

Deputy Secretary of State Warren Christopher entered into long and difficult negotiations to free the hostages. Iranian conditions for the release of the hostages included: 1) that the United States not interfere in the internal affairs of Iran; 2) that the United States unfreeze Iranian assets in the United States; 3) that the United States should drop any financial claims against Iran; and 4) that the United States repatriate all private assets of the Shah to Iran.[28] The fourth condition was the most difficult and the stumbling one and the two countries continued negotiating it for almost six weeks.

Frustrated over its inability to free the hostages and of Iran's defiance in ignoring their diplomatic status, President Jimmy Carter authorized a rescue mission in April 1980, but due to logistical problems, it was aborted in the Iranian desert. The failure further enhanced the extremists under Khomeini. Finally, though not before President Carter left office, Iran freed the hostages on January 25, 1981.

This hostage incident was in fact responsible, as a catalyst if not as the overall cause, for the full rupture of bilateral relations between the two countries. In the years that followed, mistrust continued to grow. To the present day, diplomatic, political, and economic relations between the two countries are on hold. There is no Iranian representative in Washington, and likewise, there is no American representative in Iran.

Militarily, the United States, first viewing a hostile Iran as a threat in Cold War terms, and then seeing its efforts to acquire weapons of mass destruction, particularly nuclear weapons as an even greater threat, sought to limit its ability to rearm itself after the long Iran-Iraq war. It warned the Russians, Chinese and North Koreans, for example, not to support a nuclear arms capability.

The United States also tracked the Iranian military ships in the Arabian/Persian Gulf region, leading to a number of incidents. In 1988, the US Navy shot down a civilian airliner with 292 passengers and crew aboard. It claimed afterward that it had mistakenly believed that the aircraft was preparing a suicide attack on US Naval shipping. All aboard the Iranian airliner were killed.[29]

Another fiasco occurred in 1985, when the United States, learning that Israel was illegally transferring US arms to Iran, tried to blackmail Tehran into forcing the release of American hostages held by Shi'ite terrorist elements in Lebanon supported by Iran. In a complicated deal, later known as 'Iran-Gate', the transfer of American weapons and spare parts would continue in return for the release of the hostages.[30]

When the deal leaked out to the media, those involved on both sides were identified and it became a scandal for Iranians and Americans alike. The media in both the United States and Iran wrote extensively about the matter, exposing the scandal to the public in both countries. As a matter of fact, the United States had been secretly supplying Iran with military hardware since the beginning of the Iraq-Iran war in 1981. The Americans announced their neutrality to the war, but they were secretly providing both sides, i.e. Iran and Iraq, with military weapons.

Economically, the United States adopted a confrontational policy toward Iran by invoking economic sanctions that prevented American companies and banks from dealing with Iran. The following reasons were given to justify the sanctions:

(a) Iran's support of terrorism and radical organizations.

(b) Iran's refusal of the Palestinian/Israeli peace process and its financial support for the Arab/Palestinian extremist organizations.

(c) Iran's interest in acquiring weapons of mass destruction, including a nuclear bomb.

All these reasons were behind the United States imposition of the economic sanctions against Iran.

Because the anti-modern, anti-Western policies of the republican government have strangled the economy, the need for foreign investment has increased, and has made American economic sanctions more painful than they otherwise might be. In recognition of this, leading reformist members of the Iranian Parliament have stated on numerous occasions that lifting the sanctions is a necessary condition for entering into a dialogue with the United States. In addition, Mr. Mohammad Reza Khatami, the brother of President Khatami has said that: "the extension of the sanctions would destroy all the bridges and all the efforts we have been making to repair relations [with the United States]."[31] These statements and others indicate how keen the reformists are to reestablish an economic relationship with the United States. The sanctions are also potentially harmful to American companies, preventing them from competing for major oil and other projects of Iran, whereas Japanese and European companies are under no such restrictions.

Relations between Iran and the United States have remained strained over three decades, with neither side willing to make necessary changes. The powerful religious conservatives, who are considered as the radical group in Iran, do not want to reestablish diplomatic and political relations with the United States. They are afraid of the American and European influence on Iranian society. In addition, they are afraid that western culture may undermine the values and the religious character that the 1979 revolution has brought to the Iranian society.

Nevertheless, there have been signs of willingness to establish some kind of relationship with the United States. As early as 5 July 1985, Mr. Hashemi Rafsanjani, who was at the time the Chairman of the Iranian Parliament, called the United States to reestablish its diplomatic relations with Tehran. Nothing came of it, but it did represent a slight change. Over the years, there have been other small gestures. Academic meetings are now common and both countries have relaxed travel restrictions on Americans visiting Iran. There is also an opportunity for low-level conversations between Iranians and Americans at the United Nations in New York. Although the Iranian Foreign Minister, who visits New York several times a year, is not allowed to visit Washington, the Iranian Minister of Finance visits Washington to attend meetings at the World Bank and other international financial institutions. In November 2000, the Foreign Minister and the US Secretary of State, meeting at the United Nations in New York, shook hands for the first time since the revolution. Resistance to resuming normal relations thus seems to be lessening in both countries. However, both governments still have mixed feelings toward that task and both parties appear to be waiting for the 'miracle' that would happen to break the ice.

CONCLUSION:

We mentioned earlier that there are many similarities in Iran's and Saudi Arabia's approaches to dealing with the United States. But there are also major differences. Whereas, the relationship between Saudi Arabia and the United States of America started from a normal, 'commercial' relationship with American oil companies and evolved over the years to a 'Strategic Relationship', Iran and the United States started with a 'Grand Strategic Relationship' and ended up collapsing. The Saudis have developed their relationship with the United States in a gradual manner, whereas the Iranians have started that relationship from the top. Therefore, the Saudi-American relationship has continued, whereas the Iranian-American relationship has not.

With the 1979 revolution, Iranian interest in obtaining economic and military aid from the United States ebbed as the new regime dedicated itself to creating a revolutionary Islamic political order at home and exporting the revolution abroad. With the end of the Cold War, American strategic interest in Iran bordering the Soviet Union receded and the importance of Iranian oil receded as well. In addition, the presence of Iran on the eastern part of the Arabian-Persian Gulf could also present another threat to many Arab Gulf countries, as well as to Saudi Arabia. The closure of the Straits of Hormuz by Iran would cause an immense disruption on the flow of Gulf oil to the entire world including the United States. The US knows that the closure of the straits would adversely affect the global economy, and that is why it must be kept open.

On the other hand, the 'Strategic Relationship' between Saudi Arabia and the United States is still very important, not only due to the potential threat from Iran, but the continuing actual threat from Iraq on its northern-eastern borders. Iraq with its military power could threaten Saudi Arabia and many other countries in the region. Therefore, the American military presence in the Gulf region is vital and important to the political stability of the entire region. Presently, she has a number of naval vessels, carriers, troops, and other facilities in the Arab Gulf countries. Nevertheless, the resumption of relations between Iran and the United States is very important for reintegrating Iran with the global economy, and for Iran to receive more international investment for economic development at home. In fact, Iran still needs the United States and the United States still needs Iran. However, the conservatives of Iran argue that they do not need the United States and the reformists argue that they need the United States.

While Iranian archconservatives say that Iran should have no dealings with the 'Great Satan', the reformists say that they would like to deal with the United States so long as it is on an equal basis. President Mohammad Khatami stated in 1998 that both countries need to start with some confidence-building measures, and could begin by creating a secret channel for opening up a dialogue through a third country. Khatami believes that there has been an essential change in the 'world order', and it is necessary to live with the realities of the new world. Moreover, Khatami does not object to the Palestinian-Israeli peace process because he does not believe that Israel would vanish in the short term. In fact, he believes that Israel, sooner or later, will recognize the Palestinian rights and will accept to live with them under their own independent State. Furthermore, Khatami gives a great deal of importance to the Saudi-Iranian relationship. He wants to build that relationship on solid bases. Likewise, he wants to build Iran's relationship with the other Arab Gulf States and solve all outstanding problems with those countries. He even believes that there is no hatred against the American people in Iran.

In December 1999, and in an Iranian stadium packed with 5000 students and academics he announced that: 'We have no hostility toward the American nation'. While a small group chanted 'death to America', the great majority of students cheered.[32] While the arch-conservatives oppose such a notion, most Iranians, and specially the younger generations appear ready to resume relations with the United States. Understanding these beliefs and feelings, one would fear that Khatami will be a target for the extremists inside Iran. He might be killed by the radicals of Iran. If this incident takes place, the reformists will face the end of their futuristic hopes.

As early as 1997, Saudi Arabia said that it was ready to mediate between Washington and Tehran. In their view, the Saudis believe that the current stalemate between Iran and the United States does not serve neither American nor Iranian interests. Despite their differences on many political issues, both, the Americans and the Iranians, share some common interests such as the removal of Saddam Hussein in Iraq and the Taliban in Afghanistan. Therefore, the Iranians should forget the tragedies of the last two decades, and the Americans should take advantage of the presence of a moderate and a reformist government in Iran. Conciliation from both sides is the only way out of their present stalemate.

In order for the reformists to succeed, however, Iran needs to change its image as a radical Islamic Republic and show the outside world that they are an open country. It will not be easy, for the conservative extremists will do everything in their power to reject any opening to the United States. If they thought that the reformists were gaining the power to succeed, it is plausible that Khatami and other reformists would become targets for the extremists inside Iran. If extremists killed leading reformists, Iran could very well remain in isolation from the rest of the world for years to come. The gains that the reformists have made would also probably be lost. Iranian open diplomacy with the outside world, which has been pursued during Khatami's ruling time, would vanish; and better treatment for ethnic and religious minorities would probably also collapse. Gone would be Khatami's dream of the unity of the Iranian people where there would be no difference between Shi'ite and Sunni or Persian and Azeri. To him, they are all Iranians and they should be treated equally.

All in all, one may conclude here that the relationship between Saudi Arabia and the United States was built and is still going on mutual respect, mutual interests, and better hopes for the future. The relationship between the United States and Iran was built on pure self-interest on both sides. The American interests during the Cold War were in making Iran a buffer to the Soviet expansion in the Gulf, as well as commercial and strategic interests in oil; and the Iranian interests were in using the United States originally to prop up the regime and then to provide arms and military training in order for Iran to gain hegemony in the Gulf region. The relationships in both cases were an outcome of the circumstances of the time. That is why the relationship and ties between Saudi Arabia and the United States survived, and the relationship between Iran and the United States did not.

It is in all three countries' interests, Saudi Arabia, Iran and the

United States, for the Gulf region to be politically and economically stable. Saudi Arabia's first priority is to develop its economy for the benefit of its society while maintaining its Islamic values. This can only be done in a peaceful and stable environment. That should be the goal of Iran also, but to achieve that goal, it must open up the country to foreign investment to create a better economic future for its people. For the United States, a stable economic and political environment is a major interest for the world's largest repository of exportable oil.

The Gulf War proved that despite the end of the Cold War, military as well as political threats endanger these mutual interests of the countries of the region. No one country can unilaterally create or maintain regional stability in the Gulf. There must be cooperation on all sides.

FOOTNOTES

(1) Ukaz Newspaper, 'The Kingdom And the United States: A Strategic Alliance', September, 5, 2000. No. 12428. P.14. See also David E. Long, 'The Unite States and Saudi Arabia: Ambivalent Allies'. Westview Press, p.13.

(2) Ibid. During the meeting, the two leaders have discussed a number of important issues including the oil issue, the Palestinian-Jewish crisis, the economic issue, the political issue, and the military issue. Other issues were also discussed.

(3) Ibid. p.14

(4) Three future Saudi Kings represented Saudi Arabia at San Francisco. Then Prince Faisal was accompanied by his two brothers, then Princes Khalid and Fahd.

(5) For more details of the Crown Prince's visit, See David E. Long, 'The United States and Saudi Arabia: Ambivalent Allies', Westview Press, p.91.

(6) The Kingdom of Saudi Arabia has given more than US$24 billion to Iraq in addition to arms and other facilities. An oil pipeline was established between Saudi Arabia and Iraq to facilitate the exporting of Iraqi oil from Iraq to the outside world.

(7) 60% of the Iraqi population is Shi'ite, and 95% of the Iranian population is Shi'ite. Moreover, 75% of the Iraqi army is Shi'ite, and 100% of the Iranian army is Shi'ite.

(8) F. Gregory Gause III, 'The U.S.-Saudi Relationship and the Gulf War' in David W. Lesch, 'The Middle East and the United States', Second Edition, Westview Press, P.348.

(9) See the documentary shown on the 'Desert Storm War', Kuwaiti TV., February 24, 2001.

(10) Saddam Hussein was forced to sign the cease fire treaty, and a number of other conditions were imposed on him such as the destruction of his long range missiles, his biological and chemical factories, and the acceptance of a UN team to investigate his compliance with all the treaty's conditions.

(11) David E. Long, Op. cit, p.117

(12) Ibid. pp.75-80

(13) Oil prices jumped from US$3.5 to US$40. The Kingdom of Saudi
     Arabia and other oil producing countries in the Arab World
     became billionaires in 24 hrs.

(14) The Kingdom of Saudi Arabia adheres to the Islamic Law
     (Shari'ah). Therefore, it would apply this law on any foreign
     citizen who breaks its laws including American citizens. The
     Americans understand this, and they always warn their citizens of
     the necessity to abide by the Saudi law.

(15) Sheikh Kamal Adham is the half brother of Queen Iffet, the wife
     of King Faisal. He was considered as one of the most faithful
     people to King Faisal. He died in 1999 in Cairo and was buried in
     Makkah.

(16) It was also said during that time that the British Intelligence
     Service (MI6) had cooperated with the Central Intelligence Agency
     in bringing back Shah Mohammad Reza Pahlavi to power.

(17) Ali M. Ansari, Iran, Islam and Democracy: The Politics of
     Managing Change, The Royal Institute of International Affairs,
     Middle East Program, p.13. In fact, Muscadel was challenging the
     British existence over the Iranian soil. He was a communist who
     wanted to turn Iran into communism. He and his supporters were
     proclaimed to be nationalists.

(18) R.K. Ramazani, 'Revolutionary Iran: Challenge and response in
     the Middle East' The Johns Hopkins University Press, Baltimore
     and London, p.202

(19) The American embassy in Tehran had more than 400 Americans
     who were serving the different interests of the United States in
     Iran and other Middle Eastern countries. As a matter of fact, the
     first American consulate in Iran was opened in 1883. Its main
     interest was the protection of American citizens living in Iran. For
     more details, see Amirah Mohammad Kamil Al-Kharbouti, 'The
     History of the American-Iranian relations (1947-1989)', First
     edition, Al-Kateb, Cairo, Egypt, p.5

(20) Amirah Mohammad Kamil Al-Kharbouti, op. cit. pp.12-13

(21) 'The Shah and I: The Confidential Diary of Iran's Royal Court',
     Introduced and Edited by: Ali Naghi Ali Khani, Madbouli Book
     Store, Cairo, Egypt, 1993, p.16

(22) 'The Shah and I', op. cit. pp.20-21

(23) David Menashri, 'Iran: A Decade of War and Revolution', Holmes
     & Meier, New York and London, p.48

(24) Ibid. p.70. The letter was not sent to President Johnson because

the private secretary of the Shah knew in advance that it will anger the U.S. President especially during that critical time.

(25) 'The short words: Preachments and wisdoms from the talks of Imam Khomeini', The Institute of organizing and publishing the legacy of Imam Khomeini, Tehran, The Islamic Republic of Iran, 1993, pp.204-205

(26) Dr. Mahdi Shahadeh and Dr. Jawad Bisharah, Iran: 'Challenges Ideology and Revolution', Center for Arab-European Studies, First Edition, 1999, p.101

(27) For more details of this incident See 'The World Almanac and Book of Facts 1982', Newspaper Enterprise Association, INC, New York, pp.824-825.

(28) Ibid.

(29) Reuter News Agency, 'The Candidate for Iranian Presidency calls for talks with Washington', 6/1/2001

(30) Amirah Al-Kharboutli, Op. Cit. pp.182-188

(31) Washington Intelligence Report and Estimates (WIRE), June 25, 2001, WIRE-1459.01, p.9

(32) Afshin Valinejad, 'Anti-US Slogans Prevented in Iran', Associated Press, December 12, 1999.

CHAPTER FIVE

RELATIONS WITH THE AFRICAN CONTINENT :1982-1997

Introduction:

Africa was not a major foreign policy interest of either Saudi Arabia or Iran until after World War II. Prior to then, both countries had cordial if not necessarily close diplomatic relations with Africa, particularly with the Arab states of North Africa and to a lesser extent with the Muslim communities in the rest of the continent.

African Muslims in Arab North Africa and sub-Saharan East and West Africa have maintained religious ties with Arabia since the earliest days of Islam since Saudi Arabia is the site of Islam's two holiest shrines, Makkah and Al-Madinah. Every Muslim who is physically and financially able to do so is required to perform the Hajj, the Great Pilgrimage to Makkah, once in his or her lifetime. Many also make the Umrah, or Little Pilgrimage, that can be made at any time during the year. In recent years the number of Africans making the Hajj has been in the hundreds of thousands. With the establishment of the Islamic republican regime in Iran following the overthrow of the Shah in 1979, Iran has also greatly increased its interest in African Muslims, albeit in a much more militant, political context.

Saudi Arabia and Iran have also increased commercial ties with Africa, particularly with oil producing states in OPEC, including Nigeria, Algeria, and Libya. Many non-oil-producing African states have been recipients of economic aid programs from both Saudi Arabia and Iran to help fight poverty, illiteracy and disease.

During the period addressed in this book, Saudi Arabia's foreign policy toward African Muslim states was based, as was its foreign policy in general, on three pillars. The first was its sense of responsibility as Custodians of the Two Holy Sites of Makkah and Al-Madinah to further the unity and welfare of the world Muslim community. This included financial aid and political support for fellow Muslims and opposition to threats to their interests. A corollary to its special concern for the welfare of the Muslim world is the requirement of all Muslims to aid those in need, Muslim and non-Muslim alike, based on the Islamic principle of Zakat (charity). The second pillar is solidarity with all Arab states which includes all the Arab African states in North and East Africa. The third pillar is to encourage peaceful commercial and political relations with all countries for their mutual benefit.

Iran is not Arab, and although its population is mostly Muslim, it was largely a secular state under the Shah. Since the Iranian revolution, however, it has shown great interest in increasing its religious and political influence throughout the Muslim world, including Africa.

Prior to World War II, both Saudi Arabia and Iran were more preoccupied with consolidating a strong nation state in their respective countries than they were with foreign policy in general, and particularly Africa. Saudi Arabia's main interest in Africa centered on the annual Muslim pilgrimage to Makkah.

Indeed, it was under King Faisal bin Abd Al-Aziz (r. 1964-1975) that Saudi Arabia became fully engaged diplomatically in the African continent. He visited the Islamic states of Africa twice, in 1966 and again in 1972, in order to promote his call for Islamic unity. He used these opportunities to urge the non-Arab Islamic states of Africa that had established diplomatic relations with Israel to sever them. In both endeavors, his trips reaped success.[1] King Faisal viewed Israel, which in 1967 occupied Al-Aqsa, the third holiest site in Sunni Islam, to be a threat not only to the Arab world, but to the Muslim world in general.

King Faisal was assassinated in 1975, and was succeeded by his half-brother, King Khalid bin Abd Al-Aziz, who ruled until his death in 1982. King Khalid was a pious man and highly respected, but he delegated the day-to-day running of the government to his half-brother, Prince Fahd bin Abd Al-Aziz, who succeeded him as King.

Iran, on the other hand, was more preoccupied under the monarchy with domestic stability and modernization than with religion and did not focus on establishing closer ties with Africa. Reza Pahlavi, the founder of modern Iran, came to power in 1921 and in 1925 deposed the Qajar dynasty and declared himself Shah. He was greatly impressed by the efforts of Kemal Ataturk to modernize Turkey after World War I, and set about to create a similar, Westernized secular state. His son, Mohammed Reza Shah, who succeeded his father in 1941, did extend Iranian relations to include Africa. However, his foreign policy toward Africa was not based on Islam, but on secular mutual interests.

With the Iranian revolution and the overthrow of the Iranian monarchy in 1979, the secular policies of the Shah, both domestically and in foreign policy, came to an abrupt end. The new republican regime, under the leadership of Ayatollah Khomeini, espoused a militant, Islamist political ideology at home and abroad, based on his revolutionary Shi'a ideology, 'Velayat-e-Faqih' (Guardianship of the Jurist). In foreign policy, the new regime set out to spread its revolution throughout the Muslim world.

This militant foreign policy was forestalled, however, by the outbreak of the Iraq-Iran war in 1980. For eight years, Iran had only one target and one enemy, and that was Iraq and the regime of President Saddam Hussein. When the war finally ended in 1988, Iran was not only devastated economically, but was politically isolated. It was demonized by the United States which it in turn demonized, calling it "the Great Satan."

During the 1990s, Iran sought to break out of its isolation and at the same time spread its militant brand of Islamic revolution. Among the first targets of opportunity was Africa. Taking advantage of a new influx of oil revenues due to a price hike in the wake of the Iraqi invasion of Kuwait, Iran set out to establish close relations with all the African states, both Muslim and non-Muslim.

Iran created economic assistance programs, emphasizing its concern for Africa's future economic and political welfare. In the early 1990s, it initiated assistance programs for African countries having difficulty raiding the foreign exchange to cover the purchase of oil. Despite Iran's focus on political and economic relations, however, its priority was always to spread its influence throughout the Muslim world and to that end it concentrated on cultural Islamic relations.

In 1992, Iran sent delegations to 24 African states, concluding different agreements in almost every area of political, economic and social relations. For the remainder of the period under study, i.e. until 1997, these efforts brought mixed results, and many of these agreements were never implemented or even respected. As will be examined below, perhaps its greatest success was the Sudan.

Bilateral Relations with the Arab-African States:

Both Saudi Arabia and Iran initially concentrated on developing closer diplomatic relations with African members of the Arab League: Egypt, Morocco, Algeria, Mauritania, Tunisia, Libya, Sudan, Somalia, Djibouti and The Comoro Islands.[2] The nature of the relations, however, differed with each country.

Saudi Relations with the Arab-African States:

Diplomatic relations between Saudi Arabia and the ten Arab-African countries have always been based on Arab solidarity and conducted with mutual respect and mutual interests. As a member of the Arab League, Saudi Arabia has always sought to maintain close, cordial relations with all the Arab states of Africa and to avoid becoming involved in bilateral tensions or disputes when they have arisen. The Kingdom has mediated a number of times in resolving the bilateral disputes and feuds between the Arab-African countries, succeeding in some cases and failing in others. The following are brief outlines of four African Arab countries with which, for a variety of reasons, Saudi Arabia has had particular interests.

Egypt:

Although Egypt was a neighbor and a major Muslim and Arab state, relations between the two countries were cordial though not close before the overthrow of the Egyptian monarchy in 1952. From then on, the relationship has been of major importance to both countries. However, the relations themselves have fluctuated from extremely cordial to confrontational.

When Jamal Abd Al-Nasser became President of Egypt in 1953, relations flourished. Nasser was hailed by the entire Arab world for standing up to British imperialism, including Saudi Arabia even though it had never experienced colonial rule. Nasser was a devout Muslim, and although his brand of Arab socialism was secular, the Saudis did not consider it incompatible with Islam. Moreover, thousands of Egyptian Muslims attend the Hajj, the Great Pilgrimage to Makkah each year, and many more make the Umrah, or Lesser Pilgrimage, usually during the holy month of Ramadan.

During the early years of the reign of King Saud, the eldest surviving son and successor of King Abd Al-Aziz who succeeded him in 1953, economic and military cooperation between the two countries greatly increased. Moreover, Egypt was seen by Saudi Arabia as a gateway to the African continent.

However, after President Nasser turned to the Soviets for military assistance in 1955, relations began to sour. For Saudi Arabia, Soviet communism represented atheism and was considered amoral as well as a political and military threat to the Muslim world. Saudi relations with Egypt deteriorated even more during the 1960s when Egypt backed the revolutionary regime that overthrew the Imam of Yemen, initiating a civil war that lasted until Nasser had to withdraw its troops from Yemen because of the war with Israel in 1967. Nasser was also a leader of the "Nonaligned Movement" that claimed to favor neither the Soviets nor the free world, but in reality focused on opposition to European colonialism.

The Saudis opposed colonialism, but feared that its anti-Western bias would weaken efforts to contain the even worse threat of atheistic communism under Soviet domination. In 1964, King Saud was succeeded by his brother, King Faisal bin Abd Al-Aziz. King Faisal knew the importance of Egypt in the political and the military arenas of the Arab World. His rivalry with President Jamal Abd Al-Nasser who ruled Egypt from 1953 until 1971 made him aware of the importance of the African continent. To counter Nasser's call for Arab unity under Egyptian leadership, King Faisal began his call for a broader unity of Islamic states in 1965.

When President Nasser died in 1971, he was succeeded as President of Egypt by Anwar Sadat who remained in that position until his untimely death in 1982. King Faisal, who had been Foreign

Minister under both his father, King Abd Al-Aziz, and his brother, King Saud, had made friends with many senior Egyptian leaders in that position, including Sadat, and the two leaders restored mutual cordiality and respect to Saudi-Egyptian relations. Following Sadat's expulsion of the Soviets from Egypt in 1972, Saudi Arabia and Egypt again enjoyed a commonality of interests. For the Saudis, Egypt again became a door to the African continent.

By 1977, relations had again cooled. President Sadat asked Saudi Arabia for one billion US dollars in financial aid to compensate, he claimed, for the rise in oil prices following the 1973 Arab-Israeli war. The Saudis refused. In the wake of President Sadat's trip to Israel in 1977 and his signing the Camp David Accords in 1978, Arab states, including Saudi Arabia, severed relations with Cairo.

In 1982, President Hosni Mubarak became President. One of his first goals was to reconciliation with the 17 Arab states that severed their diplomatic relation with Egypt after 1978, restore relations with them and reunify the Arab world. In this he succeeded. Resuming relations with Saudi Arabia was particularly fruitful, opening the door for both countries to a new chapter in their bilateral relationship. This new Arab unity was seen during the Iraq-Iran war, in which both Saudi Arabia and Egypt supported Iraq. Egypt sent workers to Iraq to compensate for those Iraqis who were sent to the battle front.

In addition, Saudi Arabia and Egypt cooperated in aiding African countries seek solutions to border disputes, such as the Libyan-Chad feud, the Somali-Ethiopian dispute, and the Eritrea-Ethiopian problem. The Saudis depended heavily on Egypt as an African state, and was consulting it in developing its own African policies. Cooperation also extended to international organizations. Both countries are members of the League of Arab States, which is based in Cairo. Both of them are also members of the Organization of Islamic Conference (OIC) which is located in Jeddah, Saudi Arabia.

Saudi Arabia and Egypt also cooperated on two major Middle Eastern problems, terrorism and the Arab-Israeli conflict. In those years, Egypt in particular was faced with the terrorist danger imposed by the different Islamist groups who waged a "war of terrorism" against Egyptians and foreigners alike. Between 1993 and 1996, around 1000 foreign tourists and Egyptian civilians were killed by members of Islamic terrorist organizations.[3] Saudi Arabia supported the Egyptian government in its fight against these groups until the late 1990s when Egypt opened negotiations with the leaders of the militant religious organizations and succeeded in reaching a peaceful solution with them.

Concerning the Palestinian question, Saudi Arabia and Egypt, despite ups and downs in their relations, have always been part of the Arab consensus that the core of the problem is the injustice done to the Palestinian people in denying them the right of self-determination at the time of the 1948 partition, although they made up 70 percent of the population of Palestine. Both countries insisted that the Palestinian people have their own independent and integrated state.

The Saudis, for example, sought to solve the Palestinian dilemma with an eight point proposal called the "Fahd Peace Plan." King Fahd bin Abd Al-Aziz presented the plan to the summit of the Arab League in Fez, Morocco on August 8, 1981 and it was accepted by all the League of Arab States members.[4] In fact, Saudi Arabia has been the greatest financial supporter of the Palestinian Authority, as well as providing political and moral support.

Egypt has also been a major supporter of the Palestinian cause, supporting the Palestinian authority politically, logistically, and morally. During the Egyptian-Israeli negotiations President Sadat asked the Palestinians to join the process and even had the Palestinian flag flown beside the Egyptian flag. Nonetheless, he could not convince the Palestinians to join him.

Strong cultural and social ties have augmented the basic commonality of interests between the two countries, particularly with western Saudi Arabia, just across the Red Sea. Both countries are overwhelmingly Sunni Muslims, and thousands of Egyptians visit the Islamic holy places in Makkah and Al-Madinah each year to perform the annual Hajj or Great Pilgrimage, or Umrah or Little Pilgrimage. In addition, many Saudis have married Egyptian wives, and some Egyptians have also taken Saudi spouses. Saudis also own homes, apartments, and farms in Egypt. Moreover, many Saudi students receive their education in Egyptian schools and universities, and there are Egyptian students in Saudi Arabia, particularly in Islamic studies. Saudi Arabia has also financed the building of a number of mosques and cultural centers in Cairo and other cities in Egypt.

Economic relations are also strong. In addition, there were some 1.2 million Egyptian workers in Saudi Arabia.[5] They included, doctors, school teachers, university professors, journalists, financial managers, and clerics. Consequently, Saudi Airlines flew more than 20 flights a day to Cairo, especially during summer time. Egypt Airline flights also come to Saudi Arabia on a daily schedule. In return, many Saudis visit Egypt on vacation each year.

Egypt was also the recipient of Saudi private sector investment in banks, five star hotels, factories, tourist cities, and industries, and also in financial aid, including loans and grant assistance. In addition, during the 1990 Iraq-Kuwait crisis Saudi Arabia erased around US $ 4 billion in loans it had extended to Egypt, which in turn deployed 32,000 troops to participate in Desert Storm, the liberation of Kuwait.[6] In trade relations, Saudi Arabia also exports petrochemical products to Egypt, and imports construction materials and agricultural products such as mangos, watermelons, bananas and other fruits and vegetables.

The Sudan:

The Sudan is geographically the largest country in Africa. With an area of 2.5 million square miles, it is roughly the size of the United States east of the Mississippi River. The capital, Khartoum, is in the center of the country at the junction of the Blue and White Nile Rivers to form the River Nile. The population, numbering around 30 million, is both predominantly Arab and Muslim, and the Sudan is a member of both the League of Arab States, and the Organization of the Islamic Conference (OIC). Roughly 90 percent of the Sudanese are Muslim, most of whom are Arabic speakers, and ten percent are Christians and animists who live predominantly in the non-Arab south.[7] About 60-70 thousand Sudanese travel to Saudi Arabia each year to perform the Hajj, and an additional 30-40 thousand perform the Umrah during the month of Ramadan. There are also around one million Sudanese people working in Saudi Arabia.

Since gaining independence from the British in 1956, the Sudan has experienced four military coups, and is still ruled by a military junta today. Consequently, the Sudanese have constantly been under the rule of its armed forces since independence.

Saudi Arabia maintained good relations with the Sudan and during the rule of Ja'far Mohammed Nemeiri, 1969 to 1985, political, economic and security and intelligence cooperation was expanded. Nemeiri was deposed in a bloodless coup in 1985 and was replaced by civilian leadership under Sadiq Al-Mahdi.

When General Umar Ahmed Al-Bashir led a successful military coup and became the President in 1989, relations began to deteriorate. Creating an ostensibly Islamic regime, Bashir introduced radical, revolutionary policies at home and abroad. He made many enemies throughout the Arab world, and established close relations with the Islamic Republic of Iran. Iran, which was looking for an Arab ally, quickly forged close relations with Bashir. Bashir accused Saudi Arabia of supporting his opponents, particularly the rebels in the south of Sudan. In 1990, he alienated the entire Arab world when broke with the Arab consensus and supported Saddam Hussein when he invaded Kuwait. Saudi Arabia reacted by cutting off all economic assistance.

Saudi Arabia was angered but not surprised by his betrayal, for from the time he came to power, Bashir had cooperated with the Iraqi government and supported Saddam Hussein's cruel and dangerous policies for the region. In return for his support, Saddam began to give financial grants to the Sudan to assist its deteriorating economy.

In 1992, Bashir began to moderate some of his policies. The Sudanese government approached the Saudis, seeking a rapprochement. The Saudis agreed but without great enthusiasm, and the Sudanese had to approach the governments of Arab Gulf countries for financial aid and assistance.[8] In late 1995, a new round of talks between the two countries was started. The Saudis had learned that Osama Bin Laden had moved from Yemen to Sudan, and they asked Sudan to return him to Saudi Arabia. The Sudanese government was hesitant to give him up due to the financial investments and agricultural projects he sponsored in the Sudan. Bin Laden, however, discovered the secret talks between the Saudis and the Sudanese about him, and fled to Afghanistan in mid 1996.[9] The Saudis, who had stripped him of his Saudi citizenship the previous year, tried to have him returned from Afghanistan but did not succeed.

In sum, Saudi-Sudanese relations, while based on mutual self interests, increased and decreased as those interests coincided and collided. The most important basis is the two countries common Arab and Muslim ties. The Sudanese need for financial support and the Saudi need to further the social and economic welfare of fellow Arab and Muslim peoples and to promote political stability and regional African and Middle Eastern security formed the basis for Saudi financial aid programs to the Sudan. But after 1989, the Sudanese regime chose to follow radical and militant domestic and foreign policies. Saudi Arabia stands ready to renew a closer relationship, but it is dedicated to evolutionary development, not confrontation.

Morocco:

Saudi-Moroccan relations have been cordial and highly cooperative since Morocco received its independence from France in 1956. Morocco is a country of roughly 175,000 sq. mi. (450,000 sq. km.) and has a population of an estimated 33 million , 90 percent of whom are Sunni Muslims. Roughly 60-70,000 Moroccans perform the Hajj each year and another 30-35,000 perform the Umrah, or Lesser Pilgrimage. Cooperation between the two monarchs as well as the two governments has accomplished many successful results.

Socially, the two countries have a sound relationship also. For example, many Saudis have Moroccan spouses. These Saudis and others own homes in Morocco and spend a great deal of time in residence there. Around 300,000 Saudis spend their summer vacations there every year.

There are also extensive economic ties. Many Saudis have large investments in Morocco, particularly in real estate. The latter include hotels, summer homes, beach apartments, and palaces. There are also commercial investments such as textile factories. There are also Moroccan trade exhibitions that are shown in different Saudi cities from time to time, and the Saudis have their own exhibit in the annual Casablanca Exhibition Ground where they show all kinds of products such as carpets, coolers, and plastic chairs and tables that are made in Saudi industries and factories.[10]

Morocco has also been the recipient of Saudi financial aid. For example, donations and grants for certain projects such as the Two Brothers University which was built by King Hassan II in Ifran amounted to $50 million. The Saudi Islamic Development Bank is also contributing to important development projects of Morocco, including housing projects, road construction and a number of major social projects.

Politically, the two kingdoms have always cooperated closely on both broad regional and international issues and on specific problems. For example, in 1986 King Fahd bin Abd Al-Aziz mediated between Morocco and Algeria to solve their border dispute. After a few days of negotiations in the border city of Wujdah, he succeeded and the two countries were able to restore brotherly relations.

In addition, Saudi Arabia fully supported Morocco's role as a conciliator in other inter-Arab disputes. Morocco hosted a number of the Arab League conferences, including "emergency conferences" to address crisis situations. Saudi Arabia backed these efforts on the part of Morocco to play the role of mediator in resolving bilateral Arab disputes with both political support and financial assistance. Morocco has also supported the Gulf states in time of crisis. For example, it sent a contingent of 1200 troops to Saudi Arabia to participate in the armed coalition that succeeded in liberating and expelling the Iraqi army from Kuwait in 1991.[11] There is intelligence cooperation between the two countries, and both are members of the Arab League, as well as the Organization of Islamic Conference (OIC).

In short, Saudi-Moroccan relations are a model for cordial, cooperative relations. The two countries never had any kind of dispute, and the leaders of the countries have always looked at each other with respect and honesty.

Somalia:

Somalia, located in the Horn of Africa, is a predominantly tribal society and Muslim in religion. Previously under the rule of two colonial powers, Italy and Britain, it gained its independence in 1969. Ninety-five percent of its population of about five million are Muslims, mostly Sunnis. In 1974, Somalia joined the League of Arab States during the rule of President Siad Barre. Although Barre was very proud of Somalia's status as an Arab country, his Marxist policies made Somali relations with Saudi Arabia difficult. Saudi overtures to induce him to moderate his radicalism came to no avail.

When the Soviets decided to abandon their patronage to Somalia and support the new Marxist regime in Ethiopia in 1978, relations again stabilized. Cooperation between the intelligence services benefited both countries, and Saudi Arabia supported Somalia in the United Nations in its confrontation with Ethiopia over the Ogaden.[12] (See below under Saudi relations with Ethiopia.)

In 1985, Barre was ousted from power by his political rivals, but no one was able to consolidate power and the country was divided. Saudi Arabia recalled its ambassador from Mogadishu, and the Somali ambassador to Saudi Arabia along with other Somali officials sought asylum in the Kingdom.

A number of neighboring countries initiated mediation efforts but none of them were successful. In 1993, King Fahd of Saudi Arabia invited all disputing parties to the Kingdom to work out a settlement. He even took them to the holy city of Makkah where they swore to work together in a united government. The rapprochement did not last long, however, and again armed struggle broke out.[13] More Somali leaders fled, including the Prime Minister, Omer Ghalib Arteh, to Saudi Arabia as tribal warfare continued.

Economically, Somalia has been a recipient of Saudi financial aid, and has also benefited from transfer payments home by some half million Somalis working in Saudi Arabia. The Somalis also used to export sheep and camels to the Kingdom, particularly during the Hajj season when livestock is sacrificed and either consumed by the pilgrims or processed and given to the needy throughout the Muslim world. In 1995, however, the Kingdom was forced to embargo livestock from Somalia. As political and social conditions deteriorated, Somali livestock became diseased, and for public health reasons, the Kingdom had no choice but to stop importing Somali livestock in order to protect its citizens and foreign visitors, particularly Hajj pilgrims. In sum, despite political differences and chronic political strife within Somalis, Saudi Arabia has continued to help a needy Muslim and Arab country both politically and through financial assistance.

Iranian Relations with the Arab-African States:

Iran's relations with Arab-African states were initially not as extensive at those of Saudi Arabia, due to its preoccupation with more local issues in South Asia and its suspicions of Arab states. However, Mohammad Reza Shah saw Egypt as the door to the African continent for Iran and established cordial ties with the Egyptian regime. He married the sister of King Farouq who succeeded to the Egyptian throne in 1936, but the marriage ended in divorce.

Mohammad Reza Shah also established relations with Morocco and developed close relations with King Hassan II, who succeeded his father, Mohammed V, as King of Morocco. Egypt and Morocco remained the two main African states with which the Shah formed the closest ties.

By 1982, Iran was preoccupied with its war with Iraq. It did, however, recognize the importance of trying to strengthen its ties with the Arab world, including the Arab states in Africa, and replaced its ambassadors from the old regime with new ones. Some of these new ambassadors were professional diplomats, but others were mullahs who wished to export Iran's Islamist revolution.. Most of the new appointees to Africa were from the ranks of the mullahs.[14]

Iran's efforts to strengthen ties with the Arab states of Africa were not greatly successful. Among the reasons for this difficulty were: a) strong Pan Arab ties of the African Arabs with the rest of the Arab world; b) a clash of Arab and Persian cultures; c) religious differences between the largely Sunni Arabs of Africa and the largely Shi'a Iranians; and finally d) the financial and economic support to many of the Arab African states from Saudi Arabia.

The greatest difficulty encountered by the Iranians, however, was the policy of the new regime during these years to export its Islamist revolution and support of Islamist terrorism. Iran particularly targeted Egypt and Algeria, both of which had Islamist oppositions groups, providing financial and logistical support to indigenous terrorist organizations in both countries.[15] Moreover, Iran did find a willing partner in this endeavor among the Arab African states, the Sudan.

The following are brief outlines of Iranian relations with various African Arab countries:

Algeria

As a result of Iran's involvement in terrorist activities, Iran's relations with Algeria rapidly deteriorated. Iran's underlying motive was to install a radical Islamist government in Algeria similar to its own. Iran also supported the ISF in the 1992 elections which the ISF won, but the government canceled the elections and aborted the polls.[16] It was then that the ISF and its affiliated organization (ISA) resorted to terrorism and violence to overthrow the regime. Iran's support of the ISF in its terrorist uprising against the government was particularly damaging with many Algerians massacred in ISF terrorist attacks. The Algerian government reacted by severing diplomatic relations, recalling its ambassador from Tehran and demanding that Iran withdraw its ambassador from Algeria.

The Iranian government could not maintain its subversive activities in the face of Algerian charges of its involvement in the domestic affairs of their country. Its efforts to change the Algerian political system having failed dramatically, Iran sought rapprochement with Algeria and in 1994, diplomatic relations were restored.

Egypt:

Following the overthrow of the Shah in 1979, Iran's new republican regime severed diplomatic relations with Egypt, not only over Egyptian support of the Shah, but also because of the peace agreement that Egypt made with Israel. Relations between the two countries deteriorated further over Egypt's support of Iraq in its war with Iran, which broke out in 1980. As a result of Syrian mediation between the two countries in 1987, Iran and Egypt resumed low level diplomatic relations, opening the door for bilateral talks on outstanding issues. Nevertheless, relations remained tense and suspicions prevailed.

Relations remained strained throughout the 1980s and 1990s.[17] Egypt accused Iran of training subversive Egyptian Islamic elements in the Sudan in order to carry out terrorist activities inside Egypt. In 1989, Egypt severed diplomatic relations with Iran, principally over providing support to militant Egyptian Islamist organizations , including the "Islamic Brotherhood Organization", the "Islamic Jihad" and "the Takfir and Hijrah" (Atonement and Migration [of the Prophet, Peace be Upon him] from Makkah to Al-Madinah). It accused Iran of providing arms and logistical and financial support to these groups as well as providing them with propaganda materials to preach their radical, militant fundamentalist ideology. Egypt had also discovered Iranian secret plans to assassinate the Egyptian Minister of

Interior and the son of the ex-Shah of Iran and his family in Cairo. Finally, Iran was recruiting Egyptians from the religious community as well as ordinary citizens to spy for Iran.[18]

The Egyptian government instituted counter-measures against Iran. First, together with the sons of the ex-Shah, they established an FM radio station called "the voice of Iranian Opposition." Its mission was to condemn the Iranian clandestine activities against Egypt and other Arab-African countries, to counter the Iranian propaganda attacking those countries, and also to enable the son of the ex-Shah to wage his own campaign against the Iranian regime.[19]

Relations continued to deteriorate following the Iraqi occupation of Kuwait in 1990. Iran strongly opposed the Egyptian deployment of troops as part of coalition forces participating in Desert Storm to oust Iraq from Kuwait in early 1991. Egypt considered the Iranian position as interference in its foreign policies, and retaliated by recognizing the son of the ex-Shah as his successor.

Iran continued to maintain a cultural center in Cairo, and both countries participated in a Shi'a-Sunni dialogue, but by the end of 1997, Iranian-Egyptian relations continued to be strained. If attaining even minimal cooperation was the standard of successful Iranian foreign policy, Iranian-Egyptian relations could not be described as successful.

The Sudan:

Iran did find one willing partner in this endeavor among the Arab African states, the Sudan. The relationship between Iran and the Sudan, which began following the successful Iranian revolution in 1979, was disturbing to Saudi Arabia. In the 1980s, both Iran and the Sudan found mutual interests to tighten their bilateral relations. Their cooperation was political, economic, military, agricultural, and cultural. They coordinated their efforts in using terrorist attacks against their enemies in the Arab and Western World. Iran also has accepted members of the National Islamic Front (NIF) for training in its military facilities.

In mid 1991, Sudanese President Bashir paid a visit to Tehran. He signed a "strategic agreement" with his Iranian counter part. According to that agreement, the two countries will cooperate in all fields including military and security affairs and intelligence sharing.[20] In the military field, Iran became the major supplier of small arms, artillery, surface-to-surface missiles and T59 Tanks. Iran also financed the Sudan's purchase of Chinese arms.   Iran also transported around three thousand Afghanis and former Arab Mujahhidin who had fought the Soviets in Afghanistan to the Sudan for safe haven and further training. A major factor behind this was to aid the Sudanese defeat the insurgency of non-Muslim southern Sudanese led by John Garang.

        As a result of these activities, the Sudan became a "kitchen for Iranian terrorism."   Iran would send terrorists to Sudan and wait for the right moment to use them. For example, at the end of May 1993, Iran sent the well-known terrorist Sabri Al-Banna (Abu Nidal) and a number of his colleagues from Iran to Sudan to coordinate its efforts to use terrorist attacks against its enemies in the Arab and Western World, who was staying in Iran before that.[21]

        At the same time, Iran also aided the Sudan in the diplomatic field. For example, it received about twenty Sudanese diplomats every year for training. The training program included instruction in political science, foreign languages, comparative religion, and secure communications.

        As the bilateral relationship grew, the Iranian embassy in Khartoum became the largest foreign embassy in the country with more than one hundred employees. The exchange of ministerial visits also expanded, and Iran also offered its good offices in mediating disputes between the Sudan and its neighbors. In 1996, it tried to mediate between the Sudan and Uganda in order to solve their outstanding border, political and diplomatic disputes.[22]

        In sum, the period 1982-1997 witnessed rapid and very close relations between Iran and the Sudan. It could very well be considered Iran's most successful diplomatic venture in Africa.

Libya:

        Libya was another Arab African State with which Iran wished to develop close relations, particularly since President Mu'ammar Qaddafi had supported the Iranian revolution 1979. Libya also shared the Iranian republic's antipathy toward monarchial regimes in the region. Moreover, in 1980, Mu'ammar Qaddafi condemned the Iraqi assault on Iran. As a result, relations between the two countries were cordial in the 1980s, but did not become very active until after the end of the Iran-Iraq war in 1988.   Relations expanded thereafter, particularly political relations. In 1995, for example, Iranian President Hashemi Rafsanjani sent his elder son, Mehdi, to Libya to mediate a dispute with Palestinian leader Yasser Arafat in which President Qaddafi was planning to expel a number of Palestinians who were opponents of Arafat. Qaddafi accepted the Iranian mediation and the Libyan- Palestinian dispute was resolved.[23]   There were limits to Iran's influence, however. In that same year, Iran attempted to mediate in a dispute between Qaddafi and his former Foreign Minister and second in power after the President, Abd Al-Salam Jalloud. In that case, however, Qaddafi refused to meet with the Iranian emissary.

Despite growing cooperation between the two countries, there were two areas in which Libya went its own way: military and cultural affairs.[24] In military affairs, Libya chose to deal with China, Russia and the East European countries, with which it had military relations established over a long period of time.

Culturally, Libya put many restrictions on the Iranian activities, particularly with universities and religious institutes, clerics and mosques. Libya wished to avoid clashes in cultural beliefs between the two countries, and at the same time, did not want Iran to try to influence the Libyan people with Shi'a rhetoric. Iran, which also wished to avoid a confrontation, respected Libyan restrictions.

While Iran made little or no headway in exporting its Islamic revolution to Libya, it did move rapidly in other directions. Beginning in 1992, Libya responded to Iranian offers of assistance and cooperation in both gas and oil production, and by 1997 Libya had received some 200 Iranian oil and gas experts and technicians. The two countries agreed to consult on price and production policies. Because both countries were members of OPEC and both were "price hawks" seeking to maximize oil prices, this was a natural area of cooperation.[25]

Iran also provided assistance in heavy construction for upgrading Libyan physical infrastructure such as sea and airport facilities, and commercial and government buildings. In 1996, the two countries signed a construction agreement, resulting in Iran sending about three hundred construction managers and laborers to Libya.(26) The volume of Iranian exports to Libya also increased in such commodities as Persian rugs and pistachios.

Tunisia:

Tunisia is predominantly Arab and Muslim, but has been for many years under largely secular rule. There have been only two Presidents since it obtained its independence from France in 1956: Habib Bourguiba from 1956 to 1987, and Zein El Abidine Ben Ali since 1987. The republican regime in Iran saw it as a major target for expanding their influence in North Africa in the 1990s, but did not succeed. Despite having diplomatic relations with Tunisia, it sought to undermine the regime by supporting the opposition fundamentalist Islamist group, the Tunisian Nahda (Renaissance) Movement (TNM), led by Rashed Al-Ghannoushi. TNM was the Tunisian branch of an old fundamentalist Islamic movement found throughout the Islamic world. It has ties with almost every Islamic fundamentalist group, including the Algerian (ISF) and the Egyptian Islamic Brotherhood. The TNM's aim was to purge Tunisia of all innovations that have crept into Islam since the time of the Prophet (peace be upon him), and to create what they believe is a "pure" Islamic state based on their interpretation of the fundamentals of the religion.

In 1990, some of the wanted members of the movement escaped to Iran. This issue led to secret talks between the two countries, but both countries did not find a solution to this problem. Moreover, in 1991, the Tunisian authority discovered that the Iranian charge d'affaires was secretly contacting the members of the movement at some of the offices of the Palestinian Liberation Front in Tunisia. He also had some meetings with them in different houses in the Tunisian city of Qirtaj along with some Palestinians. Therefore, the Tunisian government decided to send an envoy to Tehran to discuss this and other concerns.

The Tunisian envoy raised the issue of the multiple visits paid by Rashed Al-Ghannoushi and some of his colleagues to Iran. The Tunisian government had also received information that Iran planned to grant them "political asylum." The envoy said that Tunisia would consider any such action to be unacceptable interference by Iran in the domestic affairs of his country, noting that Iran had expressed the desire to improve relations between the two countries.

The Iranian envoy responded that the information was not accurate, and that Al-Ghannoushi and his colleagues would be allowed in Iran only until their visas expired. He also said that under Iranian law, Al-Ghannoushi and his colleagues were prevented from carrying any kind of political activities.[27]

Despite Iran's conciliatory response to the Tunisian demarche, Iran continued financial support to the TNM during the 1990s, and indeed provided monthly, or in some cases annual, stipends to senior TNM leaders. It also maintained contact with the militant Tunisian Student Association, often meeting Association members outside Tunisia. For example, in February 1991, Iranians met with two Association members in the city of Fez, the cultural capital of Morocco. Iran's aim was to introduce members of the Association to Iran's radical Islamist political ideology.[28] Iran also wanted to spread its Shi'a doctrines inside Tunisia, but was unable to do so, given that the country is almost totally Sunni Muslim. Thus, although neither Iran nor Tunisia wished totally to rupture relations, and although they continued to maintain normalized diplomatic relations, there was little cordiality displayed on either side.

Morocco:

Diplomatic relations between Iran and Morocco were severed soon after the 1979 Iranian revolution and were not restored until late 1991. There was only an Iranian official in Rabat to handle necessary communications between the two countries.

The reasons for the initially strained relations with the Iranian republic were numerous and complicated, but two factors stand out. First, the new regime in Iran recognized the Polisario Liberation Front (Frente Popular para la Liberacion de Saquia al Hamra e Rio del Oro). Polisario claimed to represent the peoples of the former Spanish colony of Western Sahara which Spain relinquished it 1975 and which was subsequently annexed by Morocco. Polisario renamed the territory the Sahari Democratic Republic (SADR) and set up a government-in exile in Algeria. The dispute has been going on ever since. Second, Morocco supported the Iraqi regime in the Iran-Iraq War, 1980-1988. And third, Morocco hosted the ex-Shah of Iran after his removal from power in Iran.[29]

Beginning in 1991, however, Iranian-Moroccan relations began to improve. In November of that year, a Moroccan delegation attended a conference in Tehran in support of the Palestinian people in their struggle against the Israelis. While there, the delegation encouraged Iranian government to reestablish diplomatic relations. As result, the two countries established bilateral talks, and in early 1993, the diplomatic relations were resumed.[30]

From that point on, relations continued to improve. For example, in an attempt to improve religious relations, the Moroccan King sent a letter to the Iranian President in July 1993 asking him to open a dialogue between Iranian Shi'a Muslim clerics and Moroccan Sunni clerics to discuss differences in legal interpretations in Shi'a and Sunni schools of Islamic jurisprudence (Madhahib). The Iranians, for their part, publicly acknowledged that King Hassan of Morocco was a descendent of Prophet Muhammad (Peace Be Upon him).

In the same letter, the Moroccan King has asked the Iranian President to help mediate the Western Sahara question in order to reunite Moroccan territory.[31] In addition, high level official visits were initiated to both countries, and cooperation increased in a number of areas. For example, an Iranian delegation composed of businessmen and directors of the Iranian industries visited Morocco to study the possibility of starting businesses there.[32] Morocco also sent a delegation to attend the International Exhibition of Tehran for the first time since the Iranian revolution. In the area of public diplomacy, Iranian newspapers began writing articles supporting Moroccan development plans and achievements, and praised King Hassan for his efforts in encouraging unity throughout the Islamic World and for his support of the world-wide Organization of the Islamic Conference (OIC). From the Moroccan side, there was a very dramatic shift in tone expressed in the media about the republican Iranian regime. For example, praise of Khomeini, the leader of the Iranian revolution, was also seen in the Moroccan newspapers.[33]

Mauritania, the Comoro Islands, and Djibouti:

Mauritania, the Comoro Islands and Djibouti all have Muslim populations and are members of the OIC. Iran wanted to spread its Islamist revolution to these two countries also, but the people, predominantly Sunni, were not receptive. Therefore, Iran basically ignored then, not attempting to infiltrate the Muslim communities, offer to finance the construction of mosques, schools or Islamic centers or even exchange ambassadors.

All in all, the Iranian efforts to exert influence in the Arab states of Africa were mixed. While failing to spread Shi'a doctrines, Iran was able to exert some influence through financial aid to some of the poorer states. Sudan during this period was probably their greatest success.

Bilateral Relations with Non-Arab African States:

Saudi and Iranian relations with the non-Arab states of Africa had both parallels and differences. Saudi relations were based on three primary mutual interests: Islamic ties with the Muslim peoples in sub-Saharan Africa, support for all sub-Saharan African states in their struggle for freedom and transition to independence, and most important during the Cold War years, resistance to Communism. The primary vehicle for furthering these interests was financial aid.

Religious ties have existed and expanded over the centuries. Many West African pilgrims, for example, walked across the continent, taking jobs along the way to sustain themselves, until they reached the Red Sea coast and sailed across to Jeddah and then on to Makkah. Many of them stayed months and even years to save up for the return trip. When they became independent of colonial rule, their home countries established embassies in Jeddah, then the diplomatic capital, and large consulates to serve the pilgrims.

During his reign, King Faisal (r. 1964-1975) made a number of visits to sub-Saharan Africa, and by the 1980s, Saudi Arabia had opened forty new diplomatic missions in the African Continent.[34] In addition to financial grants, the Kingdom built schools, hospitals, mosques, libraries, and cultural centers in many African and granted scholarships to African students to study in the Saudi educational and religious institutions.

By contrast, Iran paid little attention to the non-Arab African states prior to the 1980s. In the view of the Shah, Iran held few if any interests in sub-Saharan Africa. Even after the revolution, Iran had few contacts with sub-Saharan Africa. This apparent lack of interest resulted from a number of reasons. Among them were, first, that it was busy consolidating its rule at home. Second, it was preoccupied with the Iran-Iraq war. Third, it was still rearranging its political relations with many countries elsewhere, particularly the Europeans and the Asians. And fourth, it was engaged in reevaluating its relations with its Arab Gulf neighbors.

By 1990, however, Iran began its move towards the African Continent as a whole, particularly in offering financial aid to the poorer African states.

Saudi Arabia and the Non-Arab African countries:

The following are brief, representative descriptions of Saudi relations with non-Arab African countries:

South Africa

South Africa is an example of an African country with a small Muslim population, about 1.9 percent, that was a recipient of Saudi financial and political support. In a speech by ex-President of South Africa, President Nelson Mandela, he said:

"The support which our liberation struggle enjoyed from Saudi Arabia in particular, and the entire Arab World, not only helped secure the defeat of Apartheid. It brought us the opportunity to improve the lives of our people, through our reconstruction and development program. And our freedom is serving us well."(35)

Nigeria and Gabon

As with Algeria in North Africa, Nigeria and Gabon are both oil producers and members of the Organization of Petroleum Exporting Countries (OPEC), and both share common interests with the Kingdom in global oil economics and politics.

Saudi Arabia developed particularly close relations with Nigeria. It has the largest population of any African country, numbering by 1980s around 110-120 million, and had a plurality of about 40 percent Muslims. As a member of the Organization of the Islamic Conference (OIC), Nigeria was a major participant in efforts to bring unity to the countries of the Islamic World. Moreover, thousands of Nigerians traveled to Saudi Arabia each year to perform the Hajj each year - about 35 to 40 thousand - and many more who performed the Umrah (Little Pilgrimage).

Saudi Arabia and Nigeria also worked together on political and security issues. For example, senior political leaders often exchanged visits to discuss topics of mutual interest, particularly Nigerian dignitaries visiting the Kingdom. Many of these exchanges occur during the annual Hajj.[36] In addition, their intelligence services exchange information concerning the African continent and Middle Eastern affairs.

Angola

Through much of the period under discussion, Saudi Arabia opposed the communist-leaning ideology of Jose Eduardo Dos Santos, who came to power following independence from Portugal in 1975. Saudi Arabia, which has always been very strongly anti-communist, felt it had no alternative other than to support the anti-communist insurgency led by Joseph Sivimbi, which despite mediation efforts of Morocco, lasted until his death in 2002. The Kingdom provided financial and logistical support to Savimbi's National Union for Total Independence of Angola (UNITA). Nevertheless, with the collapse of the Soviet Union in 1987, Dos Santos began to moderate his policies. Thus, while Saudi-Angolan relations were confrontational during this period, Saudi Arabia did contribute to saving Angola from becoming a total Soviet satellite throughout the Cold War period.[37]

Ethiopia

With the exception of a brief period under Italian colonial rule, 1936-1941, Ethiopia is the only African country that maintained its independence throughout the European colonial period. During the 1970s to early 1990s, there are parallels between Saudi relations with Ethiopia and its relations with Angola. In 1974, Ethiopia was the victim of a Marxist coup d'etat that overthrew Emperor Haile Salassie, who had ruled the country since 1930. There followed a period of bloody political strife made worse by drought and refugee problems until 1991 when the regime was overthrown by a coalition of rebel forces, the Ethiopian People's Revolutionary Democratic Front (EPRDF). A constitution was adopted and the first democratic elections were held in 1995.

Because of the Marxist ideology of Ethiopia's regime, Saudi-Ethiopian relations were mixed. Strained relations were compounded by Saudi support for two insurgent groups, ethnic Somalis in the Ogaden and separatists in Eritrea:

During the turmoil following the overthrow of Haile Sellasie, ethnic Somalis in the Ogaden rebelled, and with the support of the Somali army, gained control of much of the region. In 1978, however, the Soviets decided to abandon their support of Somalia and instead support Ethiopia, thus turning the tide and defeating the Somalis. The conflict was formally ended with an Ethiopian-Somali agreement in 1988. During the protracted fighting, Saudi Arabia supported Somalia because the Ogaden had historically been a part of Somali territory and Somalis made up the vast majority of its inhabitants, and also because the Soviets had switched their support from Somalia to Ethiopia.

The second insurgency was over Eritrea. In 1962, Eritrean separatists initiated a war of independence from Ethiopia that lasted for three decades. Saudi Arabia also supported them. (see section on Eritrea)

Despite the ups and downs in Saudi-Ethiopian relations from the 1970s to the 1990s, the importance of Ethiopia as a populous (about 75 million) neighboring state dictated that Saudi Arabia and Ethiopia maintain diplomatic relations throughout this period.

Eritrea:

In 1952, Ethiopia was awarded federation status with Eritrea. A decade later, Ethiopia annexed it and declared it a province. In reaction, Eritrean separatists organized the Eritrean Liberation Front (ELF). The insurgency lasted over the next 30 years as Eritrean insurgents sought independence. There were ethnic, tribal and religious differences that separated the two countries: the Ethiopian ruling elite are largely Christian, although Muslims form a plurality of about 45 percent. Eritreans are mostly Muslim, although both faiths are found there also.

During this long, protracted conflict, the Saudis saw no choice but to support the Eritrean war of independence. Saudi support was secret in its first stage, but became well known in the later stages. In 1991, the Eritreans finally defeated the Ethiopians, and in 1993, overwhelmingly voted for independence in a referendum.

Tanzania:

Tanzania is another non-Arab African country with a substantial Muslim population. Its population (about 26 million in

1990 including about 97 percent of the inhabitants of Zanzibar and its two sister islands) is 36 percent Muslim, 34 percent Christian and 30 percent Hindu or animist.[38] Because of its large Muslim population, Saudi Arabia has financed a number of Islamic institutions, the largest of which is the Al-Haramayn Islamic Center in Dar Al-Salam, the capital. The center has a primary school, a high school and a health center. Relations have always been very cordial. In addition to embassies in each other's capital, Tanzania also has a consulate in Jeddah to service the large number of Tanzanian Muslims that make the annual Hajj and Umrah pilgrimages to Makkah. Many Saudis also travel to Tanzania to enjoy the game parks and big game hunting.

The Ivory Coast:

The Ivory Coast also has a significant Muslim population. Of the 17 million people, 35 to 40 percent are Muslim, 20 to 30 percent are Christian and the rest are indigenous animists. Most of its relatively large numbers of foreign workers are also Muslim. As a result, Ivory Coast has also been the recipient of Saudi financial assistance, particularly Islamic schools, health facilities and mosques in the north where there is a high concentration of Muslims.

Diplomatic relations were established in the 1970s, including embassies and an Ivory Coast consulate in Jeddah to service roughly 20-25,000 Muslim pilgrims who perform the Hajj and the Umrah[39] There is also a resident Ivory Coast representative to the Organization of the Islamic Conference (OIC) resident at its headquarters in the Kingdom.

Congo (Brazaville)

Congo (Brazzaville) also has a significant Muslim population. About 25 percent of its population of two million are Muslims and the great majority of them are Sunnis.[40] As a result, thousands of Congolese Muslims have made the Hajj each year and others perform the Umrah during the holy month of Ramadan.

The economy is relatively stable, backed by natural resources such as oil, gas, gold, copper, and zinc, and the government has built mosques and Islamic schools and an Islamic center for its Muslim citizens.[41] This program has had the support of Saudi Arabia which has provided financial assistance.

Niger:

Niger is one of the poorest countries in the world. About 80 percent of its 11.6 million people are Muslim. Most of the population subsist on an agrarian economy that is often subject to droughts, making them vulnerable to starvation. For these reasons, Saudi Arabia has made a special effort to provide financial and other support, and Niger's leaders have in turn sought Saudi support. Diplomatic relations are cordial. Niger also has a consulate in Jeddah to service its pilgrims to Makkah for the Hajj and the Umrah, and a representative to the OIC at its headquarters in the Kingdom.

In sum, Saudi Arabia maintained cordial relations with most sub-Saharan African states during the 1980s through the 1990s, concentrating on helping to support nation building, particularly in the poorer states, combating the spread of communism, and strengthening Islamic institutions. Its foreign aid programs were relatively successful in providing economic aid and in building schools, hospitals and Islamic institutions.

Saudi aid programs to Africa were implemented in two ways. Much of it was bilateral, directly to recipient countries. This included disaster relief for African countries suffering from drought problems and locust plagues, which devastated livestock and crops. In addition, however, it channeled financial support through the Organization of Islamic Conference (OIC) and the Islamic Development Bank. With the help of Saudi Arabia and other Muslim states, these two institutions set up a number of aid programs throughout the continent. By 1993, the OIC had channeled $3 billion to African programs.

The Kingdom also participated in mediating border and other disputes between and among various different African countries. Its overall motivation is to help the people, not to expand its own political or economic interests.

The Iranian Government and the Non-Arab African States:

It was not until 1990, i.e. after the end of the Iran-Iraq war in 1988, that Iran began to expand its relations with the non-Arab African states, particularly the poor countries. This move was a result of a number of realities. Egypt, which had formerly exerted great influence on non-Arab Africa, had turned its attentions closer to home; the United States, the remaining superpower and a check on Iran's influence, was also preoccupied elsewhere; and the most important, the Arab Gulf states, particularly Saudi Arabia, were actively involved in repelling the Iraqi invasion of Kuwait in 1990-1991.

Iran hoped to export its Islamic revolution to the African continent. In fact, much of Africa was ruled by brutal dictatorships, and military coups, regime instability and religious and tribal warfare were common. Iran saw this situation as an opportunity to help bring stability while at the same time spreading its Islamic revolution to African Muslims, particularly Shi'a minorities in countries with Sunni majorities or Muslim minorities in non-Muslim states.

Thus, the Iranian Foreign Ministry was tasked by the government to strengthen ties with African countries with significant Muslim populations. It responded by sending Iranian delegations headed by a minister or vice minister to strengthen ties throughout Africa.[42]

These delegations were tasked with the following missions: (a) to conclude trade and cultural agreements; (c) to build Islamic schools and Islamic centers; (c) to send teachers and experts to teach in these Islamic centers; and (d) to invite senior government officials to Iran. As a result, 19 Iranian delegations did visit African countries, and 18 African delegations visited Iran.[43]

Iran was accustomed to signing agreements with many countries that it did not fulfill its promises of assistance. Nevertheless, it did make a concerted effort to provide financial and technical assistance, particularly to the poorer states of sub-Saharan Africa where there were Muslim populations. Its most prominent activities were building mosques, hospitals, schools, and Islamic cultural centers and providing Islamic teachers. By 1995, it had financed 50 religious and cultural centers in roughly eighteen African countries.[44] It also sent medical doctors and agricultural and industrial experts to Africa.

This assistance was gratefully accepted by the recipients, and indeed some sought it out. For example, the Chadian Foreign Minister paid an official visit to Tehran on February, 1995. During that visit he participated in a street march with the President of Iran in celebration of the "victory day" of the Iranian revolution.[45] At the same time, he expressed his country's wish for an overall aid agreement with Iran that would include all military, economic and cultural fields, and as quid pro quo, said that his country was ready to export uranium and raw materials to Iran. He discussed military issues at more length with the Iranian minister of defense.

Thus, Iran's tactics achieved a degree of success in buying the hearts and minds of some Africans. But its actions showed that its motives were not totally altruistic. For example, the Iranian government began sending lavish gifts such rugs, furniture, and refrigerators to influential African political and Islamic religious leaders. In addition, it supported the election campaigns of local political candidates whose views it favored. In these ways, it sought to expand its ideological influence through political support as well as through its religious, humanitarian, and cultural activities. Its most prominent activities were building mosques, hospitals, schools, and cultural centers. Indeed, Iran has succeeded in extending its influence in Africa.

The following brief discussions will indicate the degree to which Iran has expanded its influence in selected non-Arab African states.[46]

Nigeria:

As mentioned above, Nigeria is the most populous country in Africa with a population at the time of about 110 to 120 million, about 40 percent of which were Muslims. Although Nigerian Muslims are mainly Sunnis, Iran has achieved a degree of influence and cordial political relations in addition to oil relations as a fellow OPEC member. It has also increased bilateral trade with Nigeria.

Culturally, it has established a Persian language chair at Ahmed Ubello University and sponsored the building of a number of cultural and Islamic centers.

Ghana:

About 16 percent of Ghana's population are Muslims, and while Iran failed to make headway in spreading its revolution, it did succeed in making some headway in exerting influence. In 1990, Iran built a hospital in the capital, Accra, which is staffed by some 30 Iranian doctors and technicians. It also built a number of cultural and Islamic centers. In addition, it created a net of intelligence personnel who are routinely in touch with Ghanaian collaborators.

Burkina Faso:

About half of Burkina Faso's population are Muslims, but Iran had little success in spreading Shi'a doctrines. On the other hand, although high population density has retarded economic development, Iran has increased bilateral trade relations, including exporting automobiles and other industrial goods for phosphate and possibly uranium. In addition, about 50 students attend Iranian universities.

Zambia:

Zambia has a significant Muslim minority of between a fifth to a third of the population. The population in the 1970s to 1990s was between six and seven million. Copper mining is the backbone of the economy, but following a collapse of world copper prices in the mid-1970s, the country went from one of the most prosperous countries in Africa to one of the poorest.

During the period under discussion, Iran made modest progress in establishing closer relations with Zambia, building cultural and religious centers for Muslims and promoting closer political and economic ties. In 1991, Iran agreed to build a military electronics plant in Zambia, as well as providing the Zambian military with small arms and sending an Iranian training mission to Zambia to train Zambian presidential security forces.

Uganda:

Uganda is another country where Iran made modest gains even though it has a relatively small Muslim though increasing population. In the 1980s and 1990s, only about five percent of Uganda's population were Muslim. In the 1990s, Iran signed cultural, economic and trade, and military agreements with Uganda and built a cultural and Islamic center in Kampala, the capital. About 350 Ugandan soldiers were sent to Iran to receive military training. There was also an exchange of scientific and oil technicians.

Tanzania:

With a substantial Muslim population, Tanzania was another target country for Iran's policy of expanding its influence in Africa, and it achieved modest success. Various bilateral committees were created to deal with cultural, military, security, and economic issues. Relations have been cordial, including a visit by the Tanzanian Prime Minister (a Christian) in 1994 who expressed strong friendship for Iran.

In cultural affairs, Tanzania's minority Shi'a community asked the Iranian government to appoint a qualified Shi'a cleric to guide the community in the observance of their religious activities. Hujjatul-Islam Minhaj was appointed in that post. The two countries signed an economic agreement in 1989, and Tanzania also signed a five year agreement to import Iranian oil in 1990.

CONCLUSION:

This chapter has dealt with the relations of Saudi Arabia and Iran toward the African continent over the period 1972 to 1997. From the perspective of Saudi-Iranian relations, it was a period of intense competition, but the competition was not aimed at confronting each other in Africa. Each country was seeking to further its own vision for the welfare all Africans, and particularly the "Umma," or Muslim community there. There were striking similarities in the visions of both countries, particularly in their mutual stress on Islamic values and on aid to less fortunate African societies. There were also striking differences in their strategies and priorities. Yet despite the fact that the two countries competed vigorously to reach their goals and targets on the African continent, neither sought to do so to the detriment of the other.

Throughout the 1970s, 80s and 90s, Saudi Arabia, despite many crises that from time to time preoccupied its foreign economic, political and security policies elsewhere, focused in Africa on strengthening Islamic values as its primary goal. Its efforts to combat communist influence and gain support for the Palestinian cause were not so much nationalistic as they were religious in nature - to safeguard people of the Islamic world and the non-Islamic Free World.

Therefore, it did not try to put conditions on its assistance to the African countries or to use any kind of pressure on them. Indeed, the African countries themselves were aware of the non-conditional nature of Saudi assistance. For the last quarter of the 20th century, therefore, Saudi relations with Africa, despite the periodic bilateral strains and differences mentioned above, remained basically positive and non-confrontational.

Iranian relations with African states also had ups and downs, and on the whole could be described as volatile. Iran's diplomatic overtures were conducted more on the basis of mutual give and take. Thus, the Iranians placed conditions on their aid and assistance

133

programs, as could be seen in their agreements and treaties, whereas the Saudis avoided imposing conditions. Iran signed more bilateral agreements with the African countries, therefore, but many of them were never implemented.

Iran was most successful in its aid and support programs - financial aid, technical, educational and military training, and in bilateral trade agreements where applicable. It was least successful in seeking to spread its revolutionary vision of Islam, its Shi'a doctrine, and to increase its political influence throughout African Muslim communities. There is no doubt that the Iranians worked very hard to reach the hearts and minds of the African peoples, particularly in the African-Arab states such as Sudan and Morocco. But they did not succeed. They also supported violent Islamist groups in seeking to attain their goals, but these efforts proved equally unsuccessful.

In sum, while the two countries chose different strategies to attain different foreign policy visions in support of their national interests in Africa, and while both countries experienced successes and setbacks, Saudi policies of offering aid and support without conditions proved to be the more effective.

FOOTNOTES

(1) As the site of the Islamic holy places, Saudi Arabia and its predecessor states have had close relations with African Muslims for centuries. However, the visit of King Faysal to a number of African states in the 1960s heralded the establishment of formal diplomatic relations throughout the African continent that have continued to expand and improve since that time.

(2) There are fifty one (51) countries in the African Continent. Ten of these countries are Arab.

(3) "Niger," in The Islamic World in Perspective, (Oxford Analytica Ltd., May 1997), pp 61-63.

(4) Boutros Boutros-Ghali, "The Foreign Policy of Egypt in the Post-Sadat Era," in Foreign Affairs, (Spring 1982), p.776. In fact, the King wanted to counter the Sadat Camp David accords and have a plan that all Arab states would accept.

(5) "Egypt," in The Islamic World in Perspective, (Oxford Analytica Ltd., May1997), p.62.

(6) Ibid.

(7) Ibid. p. .66-71, 74.

(8) Personal interview with a Saudi intelligence officer, Jeddah, Saudi Arabia, February 1997.

(9) Ibid. See also, Bill Clinton, My Life, (New York: Alfred A. Knoph, 2004), pp.797-799.

(10) There are over 2000 industries and factories in the Kingdom, located in the major cities throughout the country.

(11) An interview with a Saudi Intelligence officer who did not want his name to be mentioned. The interview took place in Jeddah, Saudi Arabia in February 1997.

(12) Al-Siassa Al-Dawlia, a monthly journal issued by Al-Ahram newspaper, July 1994, pp. 372-374.

(13) An interview with an Eriterian diplomat in Saudi Arabia. The interview took place in Riyadh, March 1997.

(14) In late 1997, the number of resident Iranian Ambassadors in Africa had reached twenty five(25), accredited to 40 countries.

(15) Personal interview in London, March,2,1989.

(16) Centre for Arab and Iranian Studies (CAIS,Ltd.), Report No. 5301/F115, February 2, 1992.

(17) CAIS Ltd., Report No. 9238/F115, August 4 1997.

(18) CAIS Ltd., Report No. 798B/F115, October 23,1990.

(19) Ibid.

(20) Personal interview, Saudi Arabia, December 10, 1991.

(21) Ibid.

(22) Ibid.

(23) Mehdi Hashemi Rafsanjani and the son of Mu'ammar Al-Qaddafi are business partners in a company registered in Malta that engages in trade activities in Africa and Eastern Europe.

(24) CAIS Ltd., Report No.798B/F115, October 23,1990.

(25) Before 1997, there were approximately 100 Iranian experts and technicians in the Libyan oil fields and in industries in Tripoli, Benghazi, and Sabha.

(26) Iran has a special organization to undertake construction projects in Africa, including Libya.

(27) An interview with a private source who did not want his name to be mentioned. The interview took place in Jeddah, Saudi Arabia on December 10,1991.

(28) Ibid.

(29) CAIS Ltd., Report No.5207/F115, November20,1991.

(30) CAIS Ltd., Report No.6031/F115, August 17,1993.

(31) Iran has also accepted a number of students from the Saharan Democratic Republic at Iranian universities and Islamic institutes.

(32) The Iranian delegations to Morocco could not find profitable projects since Moroccan laws for foreign investment and industrial conditions were very restrictive.

(33) CAIS Ltd., Report No. 6089/F115, September 29,1993.

(34) Amir Taheri, www.african-geopolitics.org/show.aspx Article ld-3114, January 17, 2005.

(35) Iqbal Jhazbhay, South African-Middle East Relations,WWW.Nurudeen.com. The speech was made on September 24,1997, in Cape Town, South Africa, in presence of Prince Sultan Bin Abd-Al-Aziz, the Saudi Defence Minister.

(36) Personal interview with a senior Saudi Hajj official, Jeddah, June,15,1986.

(37) Personal interview with a senior Saudi Intelligence official, October 5,1985.

(38) Sayed Abd-Almajeed Baker, "Tanzania," in the Islamic World League Monthly, 2nd. edition, (June 1985), pp. 103-104, 114.

(39) "Ivory Coast," in The Islamic World in Perspective, Oxford Analytica Ltd., May 1997, pp. 296, 302.

(40) "Congo-Brazzaville," in The Islamic World in Perspective, Ibid., pp.219-223.

(41) Ibid.

(42) Al-Moujez an Iran (Iran Briefing), CAIS, Ltd., September, 1999, Vol.9-No.1, Serial No.96, p.5

(43) CAIS, Ltd., Report No.4719/F115, November 5. 1990.

(44) CAIS, Ltd., Report No. 6702/F111, February 14, 1995.

(45) Ibid.

(46) CAIS, Ltd., Report No.711B/F115, July 31,1990.

Al-`Arabiyah and Farsi Islands Agreement (1968 AD)

Agreement concerning the sovereignty over the islands of Al-'Arabiyah and Farsi and the delimitation of the boundary line separating submarine areas between the Kingdom of Saudi Arabia and Iran (with exchanges of letters, map and English translation),
24 October 1968

The Royal Government of Saudi Arabia, represented by His Excellency Shaikh Ahmed Zaki Yamani, Minister of Petroleum and Mineral Resources, of the one part and the Imperial Government of Iran, represented by His Excellency Dr. Manoochehr Eghbal, Chairman of the Board and General Managing Director of the National Iranian Oil Company, of the other part.

Desirous of resolving the difference between them regarding sovereignty over the islands of Al-'Arabiyah and Farsi and

Desirous further of determining in a just and accurate manner the boundary line separating the respective submarine areas over which each party is entitled by international law to exercise sovereign rights.

Now therefore and with due respect to the principles of the law and particular circumstances,

And after exchanging the credentials, have agreed as follows:

Article 1

The Parties mutually recognize the sovereignty of Saudi Arabia over the islands of Al-'Arabiyah and of Iran over the island of Farsi. Each island shall possess a belt of territorial sea twelve nautical miles in width, measured from the line of lowest low water on each of the said islands. In the area where these belts overlap, a boundary line separating the territorial seas of the two islands shall be drawn so as to be equidistant throughout its length from the lowest low water lines on each island.

Article 2

The boundary line separating the submarine areas which appertain to Saudi Arabia from the submarine areas which appertain to Iran shall be a line established as hereinafter provided. Both Parties mutually recognize that each possesses over the seabed and subsoil of the submarine areas on its side of the line sovereign rights for the purpose of exploring and exploiting the natural resources therein.

Article 3

The boundary line referred to in article 2 shall be:

(a) Except in the vicinity of Al-'Arabiyah and Farsi, the said line is determined by straight lines between the following points whose latitude and longitude are specified hereinbelow:

Point	North latitude	East longitude
1	27°10.0'	50°54.0'
2	27°18.5'	50°45.5'
3	27°26.5'	50°37.0'
4	27°56.5'	50°17.5'
5	28°08.5'	50°06.5'
6	28°17.6'	49°56.2'
7	28°21.0'	49°50.9'
8	28°24.7'	49°47.8'

Saudi-Iranian Relations, 1982 - 1997

9	28°24.4'	49°47.4'
10	28°27.9'	49°42.0'
11	28°34.8'	49°39.7'
12	28°37.2'	49°36.2'
13	28°40.9'	49°33.5'
14	28°41.3'	49°34.3'

(b)   In the vicinity of Al-'Arabiyah and Farsi, a line laid down as follows:

At the point where the line described in paragraph (a) intersects the limit of the belt of territorial sea around Farsi, the boundary shall follow the limit of that belt on the side facing Saudi Arabia until it meets the boundary line set forth in article 1 which divides the territorial sea of Farsi and Al-'Arabiyah; thence it shall follow that line easterly until it meets the limit of the belt of territorial sea around Al-'Arabiyah; thence it shall follow the limit of that belt on the side facing Iran until it intersects again the line described in paragraph (a).

The map prepared by the A.M. Service Corps of Engineers U.S. Army compiled in 1966 was used and shall be used as the basis for the measurement of the co-ordinates described above and the Boundary Line is illustrated in a copy of the said map signed and attached hereto.

Article 4

Each Party agrees that no oil drilling operations shall be conducted by or under its authority within a zone extending five hundred (500) metres in width in the submarine areas on its side of the Boundary Line described in article 3, said zone to be measured from said boundary.

Article 5

This Agreement is done in duplicate in the Arabic and Persian languages, both texts being equally authentic. An English translation thereof is also signed by both Parties and annexed thereto.

This Agreement shall enter into force upon the date of exchange of the instruments of ratification which shall take place at Jeddah as soon as possible.

IN WITNESS WHEREOF, the above-named plenipotentiaries, duly authorized by their respective Governments, have signed this Agreement.

DONE at Teheran, this Second day of Sha'ban, 1388 (Hejira calendar), corresponding to the Second day of Aban, 1347 (Iranian calendar), and to the Twenty Fourth day of October 1968.

EXCHANGES OF LETTERS

Ia

Your Excellency:

With reference to the offshore boundary agreement signed by us today (hereinafter referred to as "the Agreement") on behalf of our respective Governments, I have the honour to propose the following technical arrangement to facilitate the determination of geographical locations offshore in the Marjan-Fereydoon area:

As soon as possible after the entry into force of the Agreement a joint technical committee of four members shall be established composed of two experts appointed by each Government. This committee shall be charged with establishing agreed positions defined by co-ordinates of latitude and longitude with reference to the map attached to the Agreement, for the following offshore at which tangible markets of various kinds already exist:

page 3| Delimitation Treaties Infobase | accessed on 18/03/2002

On the Iranian Side:

1. The well site known as Fereydoun 3
2. The well site known as Fereydoun 2

On the Saudi Arabian Side:

3. The well site known as Fereydoun 7, or in case there shall be no tangible markets therein, the well site known as Marjan 1. It is understood that whenever a new well is drilled on the Saudi Arabian side with tangible markets on it and conveniently close to the boundary line, such a well shall also be included in the reference points, thus making the number of the reference points four altogether.

The positions for these points fixed by the committee shall be regarded as accepted by both Governments if neither Government objects within one month after the committee has presented its reports, which report shall be submitted to both Governments on the same date.

Thereafter, for all purposes arising under the Agreement positions for oil operations in the Marjan-Fereydoon area carried on under the authority of either Government shall be established by reference to these points in accordance with standard survey techniques.

If the foregoing proposal is acceptable to Your Excellency, this letter and your reply to that effect shall constitute an agreement between our respective Governments, effective on the date on which the Agreement comes into force.

With assurance of my high esteem.

Teheran on 2nd Sha'ban 1388 corresponding to 2nd Aban 1347 and 24 October 1968

For the Royal Government of Saudi Arabia:
Ahmed Zaki Yamani
Minister of Petroleum and Mineral Resources

His Excellency Dr. Manoochehr Eghbal
Chairman of the Board and General Managing
 Director of the National Iranian Oil Company
 and Representative of the Imperial Government of Iran

IIa

Your Excellency:

I have the honour to inform Your Excellency that I have received Your Excellency's letter of the following text:
[See letter Ia]

I have the pleasure to convey to Your Excellency my Government's approval of the contents of your letter, the text of which is hereabove stated, considering that the letter and my reply thereto shall constitute an agreement between our respective Governments, effective on the date on which the Agreement comes into force.

With renewed assurance of my high esteem.

Teheran on 2nd Sha'ban 1388 corresponding to 2nd Aban 1347 and 24 October 1968.

For the Imperial Government of Iran:

page 4| Delimitation Treaties Infobase | accessed on 18/03/2002

Dr. Manoochehr Eghbal
Chairman of the Board and General Managing
  Director of the National Iranian Oil Company

His Excellency Ahmed Zaki Yamani
Minister of Petroleum and Mineral Resources
Representative of the Royal Government
  of Saudi Arabia

Ib

Your Excellency:

With reference to the offshore boundary agreement signed by us today on behalf of our respective Governments. I have the honour to propose, for the more effective implementation of this Agreement (hereinafter referred to as "the Agreement") the following understandings:

(a)　The oil drilling operations which are prohibited by article 4 of the Agreement within the zone therein described (hereinafter referred to as "the Prohibited Area") shall include exploitation carried out directly from the Prohibited Area and shall also extend to all drilling operations which could be carried out within the Prohibited Area from installations which are themselves located outside it.

The term "oil drilling operations" as used in article 4 of the Agreement shall mean drilling operations for oil and/or gas.

Our two Governments shall ensure that the wells drilled in the immediate vicinity of the Prohibited Area shall be vertical wells; however, when a deviation is technically inevitable at a reasonable cost. such a deviation shall not be deemed as encroachment on the Agreement, provided that the party concerned does not contemplate. by such deviation. the violation of the provisions set forth in the Agreement and this letter.

Should our two Governments mutually agree that gas injection and/or drilling an observation well is technically beneficial and advisable for the Marjan-Fereydoon reservoir. our two Governments shall agree on the location. the conducting of drilling the wells and their operations in the Prohibited Area for the sole purpose specified in this paragraph, provided that the wells to be drilled shall be conducted by each Government. directly or through its authorized agent. on its respective side of the Prohibited Area under the terms and condition to be agreed upon by our two Governments.

(b)　Our two Governments shall. directly or through authorized agents. exchange with each other all obtained directional survey information during the course of drilling operations carried out as from the effective date of the Agreement within two kilometres of the Boundary Line. This exchange shall be made on a reciprocal and continuous basis.

(c)　Each Government shall ensure that the companies operating under its respective authority shall not carry out operations that may, for technical inconsistency with the conservation rules according to sound oil industry practice. be considered harmful to the oil and gas reservoir in the Marjan-Fereydoon area.

This letter and Your Excellency's reply thereto shall constitute an agreement between our respective Governments. to become effective on the date on which the Agreement enters into force.

With renewed assurance of my high esteem.

Teheran on 2nd Sha'ban 1388 corresponding to 2nd Aban 1347 and 24 October 1968.

For the Royal Government of Saudi Arabia:
Ahmed Zaki Yamani
Minister of Petroleum and Mineral Resources

His Excellency Dr. Manoochehr Eghbal
Chairman of the Board and General Managing
 Director of the National Iranian Oil Company
 and Representative of the Imperial Government of Iran

IIb

Your Excellency:

I have the honour to inform Your Excellency that I have received Your Excellency's letter of the following text:

[See letter IIa]

I have the pleasure to convey to Your Excellency my Government's approval of the contents of your letter. the text of which is hereabove stated, considering that the said letter and my reply thereto shall constitute an agreement between our respective Governments, effective on the date on which the Agreement comes into force.
With renewed assurance of my high esteem.

Teheran on 2nd Sha'ban 1388 corresponding to 2nd Aban 1347 and 24 October 1968.

For the Imperial Government of Iran:
Manoochehr Eghbal
Chairman of the Board and
General Managing Director of the
National Iranian Oil Company

His Excellency Shaikh Ahmed Zaki Yamani
Minister of Petroleum and Mineral Resources
 and Representative of the Royal Government
 of Saudi Arabia

ATIEH
ASSOCIATES

LAW FIRM

IRAN – SOUTH AFRICA BILATERAL INVESTMENT TREATY

Official Gazette of the Islamic Republic of Iran No., 16244 Dated Nov. 28, 2000, Page 2.

Notice no.: GH-313
Notice date: Nov. 14, 2000

**To: Hojjatoleslam Excellency Seyed Mohammad Khatami
Honorable President of the Islamic Eepublic of Iran**

The Bill no. 21649/58730 dated Aug. 6,2000 of the Government concerning the Agreement on Reciprocal Promotion and Protection of Investments between the Government of the Islamic Republic of Iran and the Government of the Republic of South Africa approved at the open session of the Islamic Consultative Assembly on Tuesday 31 October 2000 and duly confirmed by the Council of Guardians, is hereby attached in application of the article 123 of the Constitution.

Speaker of the Islamic Consultative Assembly – Mehdi Karroubi.

****

No.:   37267
Date: 20.11.2000.

To: the Ministry of Economic Affairs and Finance.

The Law of Agreement on Reciprocal Promotion and Protection of Investments between the Government of the Islamic Republic of Iran and the Government of South Africa, approved at the open session of the Islamic Consultative Assembly on Tuesday 31 October 2000 and duly confirmed by the Council of Guardians on Nov. 4, 2000 and received by the letter no. G-313 dated Nov. 14, 2000 is hereby notified for execution.
Seyed Mohammad Khatami, the President of the Republic.

****

Law of Agreement on Reciprocal Promotion and Protection of Investments Between the Government of the Islamic Republic of Iran the Government of the Islamic Republic of Iran the Government of the Republic of South Africa.

Single Articles- The Agreement on Reciprocal Promotion and Protection of Investments between the Government of the Islamic Republic of Iran and the

1st Floor, Building No.74, Argentine Square, Tehran 15139, Iran — Telephone: +9821-872-1112   Fax: +9821-872-0077
E-mail: info@atiehassociates.com --- www.atiehassociates.com

145

ATIEH
ASSOCIATES
—————————————
LAW FIRM

Government of the Republic of South Africa including a preamble and fifteen articles and a protocol is approved as hereto attached and authorization is issued for negotiation of ratification documents.

In the Name of God the Beneficent the Merciful

Agreement on Reciprocal Promotion and Protection of Investments between the Government of the Islamic Republic of Iran and the Government of the Islamic Republic of Iran and the Government of the Republic of South Africa.

Preamble
The Government of the Islamic Republic of Iran and the Government of the Republic of South Africa hereinafter jointly referred to as the "Contracting Parties" and each in the singular as a "Contracting Party"

Desiring to intensify the economic cooperation to the mutual benefit of both States;

Intending to utilize their economic resources and potential facilities in the area of investments as well as to create and maintain favorable conditions for investments of the investors of the Contracting Parties in each others' territory and;

Recognizing the need to promote and protect investments of the investors of the Contracting Parties in each others' territory;

Have Agreed as follows:

Article 1- Definitions: For the purpose of this Agreement, the meanings of the terms used herein are as follows:
1.   The term "investment" refers to every kind of property or asset invested by the investors of one Contracting Party in the territory of the other Contracting Party in accordance with the laws and regulations of the other Contracting Party (hereinafter referred to as the host Contracting Party), including the following:

a) movable and immovable properties as well as rights related thereto;
b) shares or any kind of participation in companies;
c) money and receivables;
d) industrial and intellectual property rights such as patents, utility models, industrial designs or models, trade marks and names, know-how and goodwill;
e) rights to search for, extract or exploit natural resources;

1ˢᵗ Floor, Building No.74, Argentine Square, Tehran 15139, Iran— Telephone: +9821-872-1112   Fax: +9821-872-0077
E-mail: info@atiehassociates.com --- www.atiehassociates.com

Any change in the form in which assets are invested, subject to the approval of the competent authorities of the country in whose territory the investments is made, does not affect their character as investments.

2.   The term "investors" refers to the following persons who invest in the territory of the other Contracting Party within the framework of this Agreement:

a) natural persons who, according to the laws of either Contracting Party, are considered to be its nationals and do not have the nationality of the host Contracting Party.
b) legal persons of either Contracting Party which are established under the laws of that Contracting Party and their headquarters or their real economic activities are located in the territory of that Contracting Party.

3.   The term "proceeds" refers to the amounts legally yielded by an investment including profit derived from investments, dividends, royalties and fees.

4.   The term "territory" refers to areas under the sovereignty or jurisdiction of either Contracting Party, as the case may be, and includes their maritime areas.

Article 2 – Promotion of Investments

1.   Either Contracting Party shall encourage its investors to invest in the territory of the other Contracting Party.

2.   Either Contracting party shall, within the framework of its laws and regulations, create favorable conditions for attraction of investments of investors of the other Contracting Party in its territory.

Article 3- Admission of Investments

1.   Either Contracting Party shall admit investments of natural and legal persons of the other Contracting Party in its territory in accordance with its laws and regulations.

2.   When an investment is admitted, either Contracting Party shall, in accordance with its laws and regulations, grant all necessary permits for the realization of such an investment.

Article 4 – Protection of Investments

1.   Investments and proceeds of investors of either Contracting Party effected within the territory of the other Contracting Party, shall receive the host Contracting Party's full legal protection and fair treatment not less favorable than that accorded to its own investors or to investors of any third state who are in a comparable situation.

2.   If a Contracting Party has accorded or shall accord in future special advantages or rights to its own investors or to investors of any third state by virtue of an existing or future agreement establishing a free trade area, a customs union, a common market or a similar regional institution or by virtue of any domestic legislation relating wholly or mainly to taxation, or by virtue of an agreement on the avoidance of double taxation, it shall not be obliged to accord such advantages or rights to investors of the other Contracting Party.

Article 5 – More Favorable Provisions

Notwithstanding the terms set forth in this Agreement, more favorable provisions which have been or may be agreed upon by either of the Contracting Parties with an investor of the other Contracting Party are applicable.

Article 6 – Expropriation and Compensation

1.   Investments of investors of either Contracting Party shall not be nationalized, confiscated, expropriated or subjected to similar measures by the other Contracting Party unless if such measures are taken for public purposes, in accordance with due process of law, in a non-discriminatory manner and upon payment of prompt, effective and appropriate compensation.

2.   The amount of compensation shall be equivalent to the value of the investment immediately before the action of nationalization, confiscation or expropriation was taken.

Article 7 – Losses

1.   Investors of either Contracting Party whose investments suffer losses due to any armed conflict, revolution or similar state of emergency in the territory of the other Contracting Party shall not be accorded by the other Contracting Party treatment to less favorable than that accorded to its own investors or to investors of any third country.

2.   Without derogating from the provisions of paragraph (1) of this Article, investors of one Contracting Party who in any of the situations referred to in that paragraph suffer losses in the territory of the other Contracting party resulting from:

a) requisitioning of their property by the forces or authorities of the latter Contracting Party, or
b) destruction of their property by the forces or authorities of the latter Contracting Party, which was not caused in combat action or was not requied by the necessity of the situation, shall be accorded restitution or adequate compensation.

Article 8 – Capital Return & Transfer

1.   Each Contracting Party shall, in accordance with its laws and regulations, permit in good faith the following transfers related to investments referred to in this Agreement, to be made freely and without delay out of its territory:

a) Proceeds;
b) Sums derived from the sale or liquidation of all or part of an investment;
c) Royalties and fees related to agreements on technology transfer;
d) Sums paid pursuant to Articles 6 and / or 7 of this Agreement;
e) Loan installments related to an investment provided that they are paid out of such investment activities;
f) Monthly salaries and wages received by the employees of an investor who have obtained in the territory of the host Contracting party, the corresponding work permits related to that investment;
g) Payments arising from a decision of the authority referred to in Article 12.

2.   The above transfers shall be effected in a convertible currency and at the current rate of exchange in accordance with the exchange regulations prevailing on the date of transfer.

3.   The investor and the host Contracting Party may agree otherwise on the mechanism of return or transfers referred to in this Article.

1st Floor, Building No.74, Argentine Square, Tehran 15139, Iran— Telephone: +9821-872-1112   Fax: +9821-872-0077
E-mail: info@atiehassociates.com --- www.atiehassociates.com

LAW FIRM

Article 9 – Subrogation

If a contracting Party or its designated agency, within the framework of a legal system, subrogates an investor pursuant to a payment made under an insurance or guarantee agreement against non-commercial risks:

a) Such subrogation shall be recognized by the other Contracting Party,
b) The subrogee shall not be entitled to exercise any rights other than the rights which the investor would have been entitled to exercise;
c) disputes between the subrogee and the host Contracting Party shall be settled in accordance with Article 12 of this Agreement.

Article 10 – Observance of Commitments

Either Contracting Party shall guarantee the observance of the Commitments it has entered into through this Agreement with respect to investment of natural or legal persons of the other Contracting Party.

Article 11 – Scope of the Agreement

This Agreement shall apply to investments approved by the competent authorities of the host Contracting Party.

The Competent authority in the Islamic Republic of Iran is the Organization for Investment and Economic and Technical Assistance of Iran.

This Agreement shall also, subject to the approval of the competent authority of the Contracting party in whose territory the investment is made, be applicable to the investments made before the date of entry into force of this Agreement, but shall not apply to any dispute which arose before entry into force of this Agreement.

Article 12 – Settlement of Disputes Between a Contracting Party and an investor of the other Contracting Party

1.   if any dispute arises between the host Contracting Party and an investor of the other Contracting Party with respect to an investment, the host Contracting Party and the investor shall primarily endeavor to settle the dispute in an amicable manner through negotiation and consultation.

2.   In the event that the host Contracting Party and the investor can not agree within six months from the date of notification of the claim by one party to the other, either of them may refer the dispute, with due regard to their own laws and regulations, to an arbitral tribunal of three members referred to in paragraph (4) below.

3.   National courts shall not have jurisdiction over any dispute referred to arbitration. However, the provisions of this paragraph do not bar the winning party to seek the enforcement of the arbitral award before national courts.

4.   The host Contracting Party or the Investor of the other Contracting Party who desires to refer the dispute to arbitration shall appoint an arbitrator through a written notice sent to the other party. The other party shall appoint an arbitrator within sixty days from the date of receipt of the said notice and the appointed arbitrators shall within sixty days from the date of the last appointment, appoint the umpire. In the event that either party fails to appoint its arbitrator within the prescribed period or the appointed arbitrators fail to agree on the umpire, each of the parties may request the secretary General of the International Arbitral Tribunal of the International Chamber of Commerce (ICC) to appoint the failing party's arbitrator or the umpire, as the case may be. However, the umpire shall be appointed from amongst nationals of a state having diplomatic relations with both Contracting Parties at the time of appointment.

5.   The arbitration award shall be final and binding on the parties to the dispute. Each Contracting Party shall give effect to the award rendered in accordance with its laws and regulations.

Article 13 – Settlement of Disputes Between the Contracting Parties

1.   All disputes arising between the Contracting Parties relating to the interpretation or application of this Agreement shall, in the first place, be settled amicably by consultation. In case of disagreement, either Contracting Party subject to its laws and regulations, while sending a notice to the other party, may refer the case to an arbitral tribunal of three members consisting of two arbitrators appointed by the Contracting Parties.

In case the dispute is referred to the arbitral tribunal, either Contracting Party shall appoint an arbitrator within sixty days from the receipt of the notification and the arbitrators appointed by the Contracting Parties shall appoint the umpire within sixty days from the date of last appointment, if either Contracting Party does not appoint its own arbitrator or the appointed arbitrators do not agree on the appointment of the umpire within the said periods, either Contracting Party

may request the President of the International Court of Justice to appoint the arbitrator of the failing party or the umpire, as the case may be.

However, the umpire shall be a national of a state having diplomatic relations with both Contracting Parties at the time of the appointment.

2.   In case the umpire is to be appointed by the President of the International Court of Justice, if the President of the International court of Justice is prevented from carrying out the said function or if he is a national of either Contracting Party, the appointment shall be made by the vice-president of the International Court of Justice, and if the vice-president is also prevented from carrying out the said function or he is a national of either contracting party, the appointment shall be made by the most senior member of the said Court who is not a national of either Contracting Party.

3.   Subject to other provisions agreed by the Contracting parties, the arbitral tribunal shall determine its procedure and the place of arbitration.

4.   The decisions of the arbitral tribunal shall be binding on the Contracting Parties.

5.   The arbitral tribunal shall decide on the dispute according to this Agreement and the principles of the International Law.

6.   The arbitral tribunal shall reach its decision by a majority of votes.

7.   Each Contracting Party shall bear the cost of its own member of the tribunal and of its representation in the arbitral proceedings; the cost of the umpire and the remaining cost shall be borne equally by the Contracting Parties. The tribunal may, however, in its decision direct that a higher proportion of costs shall be borne by one of the two Contracting Parties.

Article 14 – Validity of the Agreement

1.   The Contracting parties shall fulfill their respective constitutional requirements for entry into force of this Agreement.

2.   This Agreement shall enter into force for a period of ten years after 30 days from the date of the last notification of either Contracting Party to the other Contracting party that it has fulfilled necessary measures in accordance with its laws and regulations for the entry into force of this Agreement. After the said period, this Agreement shall remain in force thereafter unless one of the Contracting Parties notifies the other Contracting Party in writing of its

unwillingness to continue with it, six months prior to the expiration or termination thereof.

3.   After the expiration ot the validity or termination of this Agreement its provisions shall apply to investments under this Agreement for a further period of ten years.

4.   The terms of this Agreement may be amended through negotiation between the Contracting Parties. The Contracting Parties shall fulfill their respective constitutional requirements for entry into force of any such amendments. Such amendments shall come into force by exchange of Notes between them.

Article 15 – Language and Number of the Texts

This Agreement is done in Persian and English languages, both texts being equally authentic.

Signed in Pretoria on 12th Aban 1376 corresponding to 3 November 1997 by representatives of the Governments of the Islamic Republic of Iran and the Republic of South Africa.

- For the Government of the Islamic Republic of Iran: Signed.
- For the Government of the Republic of South Africa: Signed.

Protocol

On signing the Agreement on Reciprocal Promotion and Protection of Investments between the Government of the Islamic Republic of Iran and the Government of the Republic of South Africa, the Contracting Parties also agreed on the following provisions, which shall be deemed to be and integral part of the Agreement:

Article 4 BIS

The provisions of Article 4 shall not be construed so as to oblige the Republic of South Africa to extend to investors of the other Contracting Party the benefit of any treatment, preference or privilege resulting from:

ATIEH
ASSOCIATES

LAW FIRM

1) Any undertakings it may have assumed with regard to foreign Economic development institutions.

2) Any law or other measure taken, pursuant to Article (9) of the Constitution of the Republic of South Africa, 1996 (Act 108, 1996) the purpose of which is to promote the achievement of equality in its territory, or designed to protect or advance persons, or categories of persons, disadvantaged by unfair discrimination.

This Protocol is done in Persian and English languages, both texts being equally authentic.

Signed in Pretoria on 3 November 1997 corresponding to 12th Aban 1379 by representatives of the Government of the Islamic Republic of Iran and the Government of the Republic of South Africa.

- For the Government of the Islamic Republic of Iran: Signed.
- For the Government of the Republic of South Africa: Signed.

The above mentioned Act including a single article attached to the text of the agreement consisting of a preamble, fifteen articles and a protocol has been approved at the open session of the Islamic Consultative Assembly on Tuesday 31.10.2000 and duly confirmed by the Council of Guardians on 06.11.2000.

Speaker of the Islamic Consultative Assembly: Mehdi Karroubi.

****

INDEX

Abd Al-Aziz, see also Ibn Saud, 27

Abd Al-Rahman, 27

Abu Musa, xv, xvi, 12, 17, 32

Abu Nidal Organization (ANO), 16

Accra, 130

Afghan Muslim holy warriors, Mujahideen, 40

Afghan refugees, 40

Afghan War, 38, 40

Afghani civil war, 41

Afghanistan, 8, 14-15, 37, 40, 97, 111, 118
  as a Muslim country, 8
  Communist take over, 40

Africa, 24, 42, 44-45, 60, 103-134

African High Council, 43,

African Muslims, 45

African pilgrims, 42

Ahmed Jibril's PFLP General Command, 16

Ahmed Ubello University, 130

air travel, 55, 59, 62, 110

airports,
  Dammam, 92
  King Khalid, 65
  Paris Charles DeGaul, 52

Al Khalifah, 33

Al-Aqsa, 104

Alawite, see also Shi'ism, 36

Algeria, xiv, 2, 37, 60, 80, 103, 106, 113. 115, 116, 121, 124

Algerian government, 2, 116

Algerians, struggle against the French, 31

Algiers, 2

Ali Akbar Velayati, 58

Allah, 25-26, 48

Al-Madinah, xiv, xvi, 2, 12, 25-27, 33, 66, 76, 103. 104, 109, 116

Al-Sayyidah Zainab Mosque, 36

Angola, 125

Animism, Animists, 110,127

anti-Islamic threats, 31

Arab Boycott of Israel, 5

Arab Cooperation Council (ACC), 81

Arab Gulf States, 17, 113, 129

Arab League, 19, 106, 108-110, 113

Arab nationalism, 12, 31-32, 85,

Arab socialism, 31-32

Arab states, 5, 18, 31

Arab Summit Conference in Fez, 18
  Eight-point plan, 18

Arabian Gulf Countries, 6, 32-34, 80, 95-96, 111

Arabian Gulf, 42, 53, 59, 69, 92

Arabian Peninsula, 18, 27, 30, 32, 34, 80

Arabic, 48

Arab-Israeli peace process, 18, 19

Arab-Israeli War,
  1967, 60
  1973, 60, 83